The Niger Delta

Nigeria's Broken Heart

Dr. Paul Julius

Copyright © 2016 Dr. Paul Julius

ISBN: 978-1-326-83557-6

To the beautiful ones Florence and Nicole

For their love and unflinching support

Acknowledgements

Many people contributed to the development of this book than I can possibly acknowledge. Although some of them might not agree with my interpretive arguments on the subject matter, however, their discussions or intellectual analyses inspired this book in many ways. Therefore, I will like to use this opportunity to show an expression of gratitude to them.

First are the numerous people in Nigeria including the Niger Deltans who shared their experiences with me. I spent four years shuttling between Europe and Nigeria, gathering data for this project. Everywhere I visited, I met enthusiastic people who shared their experiences with me. It is a matter of great regret that I am unable to write a more voluminous book that would have made use of all the information they enthusiastically gave. I hope they forgive me.

I also thank the entire staff and students associated with the Helen Bamber Centre for the Study of Rights, Conflict and Mass Violence at Kingston University in London, especially Dr. Andrew Higginbottom, Dr. Atsuko Ichijo and Prof. Ilaria Favretto. We spent considerable time discussing the complexities that surrounds the politics of resource governance in Africa. In these discussions, they offered invaluable insights for which I am grateful.

At the home front, I am equally grateful to my mum, sisters and twin brother - Maria, Florence, Rose, Peter and their families who were towers of strength in the difficult days. Their various points of view has been of tremendous help to this work. Peter became my research assistant during fieldworks in Nigeria. In this group is also my wife, Florence, who in the project gestation period, suffered above and beyond the call of duty. She not only acted as my in-house editor, reading and re-reading drafts meticulously, but also attended to our daughter - Nicole and postponed other important things of life.

Finally, I will like to extend my gratitude to the 'beautiful ones' (Niger Deltans) who are no longer around including my dad, Julius Aigbotsua (R.I.P). Their memories to a larger extent instigated this work. The least I can do is to dedicate this book to them all as a token of my gratitude.

Contents

ACRONYMS

AfD - Arms for Development
ARTAL - Actors, Role, Two Action Levels
AU - African Union
AFRICOM - United States Africa Command
BNAC - British National African Company
BP - British Petroleum
CBN - Central Bank of Nigeria
CDC - Constitution Drafting Committee
CHR - Commission On Human Security
COC - Council Of Ogoni Churches
COP - Council Of Ogoni Professionals
COS - Council of States
COTRA - Council Of Ogoni Traditional Rulers
DPA - Distributable Pool Account
FCT - Federal Capital Territory
FEC - Federal Executive Council
FOWA - Federation of Ogoni Women
GRA - Government Reserved Area
GWOT - Global War on Terror
HRW - Human Rights Watch
INC - Ijaw National Congress
IPOB - Indigenous People of Biafra
IYC - Ijaw Youth Council
INYM - Isoko National Youth Movement
JTF - Joint Task Force
MOPOL - Mobile Police
NDA - Niger Delta Avengers
NDDB - Niger Delta Development Board

NDVF	- Niger Delta Volunteer Force
NDPVF	- Niger Delta People's Volunteer Force
NGO	- Non-Governmental Organisation
NNOC	- Nigerian National Oil Corporation
NNPC	- Nigerian National Petroleum Corporation
NPDC	- Nigerian Petroleum Development Company
NRC	- National Republican Congress
NUOS	- National Union of Ogoni Students
NYCOP	- National Youth Council of Ogoni People
OEL	- Oil Exploration Licence
OML	- Oil Mining Lease
OPL	- Oil Prospecting Licence
OTU	- Ogoni Teachers Union
RSISTF	- Rivers State Internal Security Task Force
RNC	- Royal Niger Company
SDP	- Social Democratic Party
SMC	- Supreme Military Council
TNOCs	- Transnational Oil Corporations
UAC	- United African Company

Preface

The impetus for this factual book came from the experiences and observations made during the author's fieldtrips to Nigeria in the course of his Ph.D research. The research explored the politics surrounding the management of oil in the Niger Delta region, and how this has brought about some of the extremes in Nigeria's security complexities. This publication is an attempt to use the series of visits to the oil delta and related research to give a different perspective to what went wrong and what could be done to improve the situation. Among the issues at the heart of the conflict are youth revolts, state repression, violent militarism, acrimonious intergroup relations, mercenarism, corruption, money laundering, small arms and light weapons proliferation, and violent ethno-nationalism.

It now seems beyond contention that in the wake of over two decades of agitation and violence that has claimed thousands of lives in the oil delta of Nigeria, the region's uneasy peace has been plaqued by uncertainties, tied to the volatile political environment, the gridlocks over the passing of the Petroleum Industry Bill (PIB) at the National Assembly (federal parliament), and the proliferation of criminal activities. As it is today, militarism has eaten deep into the fabric, ethos, language and character of public discourse and action in Nigeria's oil region.

Despite the introduction of presidential amnesty on 25th June 2009 by the state to insurgents and a new government administration sworn-in on 29th May 2015, bouts of violence and extant criminalities are not uncommon in today's Niger Delta socio-political context. These intensifies regularly, following the ups and downs of the political and security processes, which has seen setbacks, new negotiations, and stalemates over questions such as resource control, federalism, disarmament of former combatants, underdevelopment and state high-handedness. The failure of the last civilian government administration (2011 – 2015) to effectively address the Niger Delta question (the president being a Niger Deltan himself), has also drawn attention to the fragility of Nigeria's democratic institutions, calling into question the political elite's ability and commitment to the Niger Delta project.

Whether this turbulence indicates that the Niger Delta region is on the brink of collapse or simply represents convulsions typical of political change in a post-conflict environment is disputed by researchers and policy-makers alike. However, to the author, the type and scale of violence and criminalities in the oil region, rooted in generalised poverty, exploitation and a discriminatory system point to a society that is fast eroding despite its enormous oil resource as a result of rising insecurity. In another sense, the 'Delta Farce has become Nigeria's Oil Mess', and the state and citizenry can only be heart-broken. But who should bear the blame?

The limits of the growth and development of most societies largely depend on the strength of the value-driven influence of their elite, and not the amount of resources as evident in the Niger Delta's case. Values such as hard-work, integrity, accountability, transparency and innovation promoted by a committed elite. The custodian elite both individually and collectively have a responsibility, an obligation to society, to plan it, organise it, order or reorder it, and above all to make sacrifices for it, for the maximum benefit of all. This is the burden of privilege placed on the elite to define clearly what is lofty, what is noble, what is deserving of honour and how these values can be sustained, preserved and enforced. To a large extent, the Nigerian political elite vacated this ethical space in its oil region and in its place are all manner of excuses and false justifications of state bad behaviour, of which societal militarisation has been the most obvious. The custodian elite in Nigeria individually and collectively failed to chart the course for the millions of people in its oil region. The elite failed to define and house the ethos and the public sense of the oil minorities. It could not define the minimum terms and conditions for the safety, security, growth and prosperity of its oil minorities in the face of global capitalist exploitation.

The result is a youth that has continued to use violence as a tool for social and political transformation, popularising it and removing it from the purview of the state. Today, violence goes beyond political and environmental motivations in the Niger Delta region, affecting the security of average individuals in the course of their day-to-day life in the Nigerian oil belt. Criminality continue to fuel insecurity at the village and municipal levels, making the centre difficult to hold. This book is not about the oil curse, but about the Niger Delta and the continuing difficulties of securing from its oil revenues a satisfactory path of economic and social development. It is a book about events where the author was born and bred, and his heart-wrenching experience on his return home.

Chapter 1 –

The Logics of Dispossession

The resurgence of low-level insurgency in the Niger Delta of Nigeria after the 2015 national elections shows the limits of appeasement that the Nigerian political elite has played in managing the oil conflict. The renewed violence and militancy in the region is proof that the country cannot continue to successfully run on a short-term solution through the assignment of tokens to aggrieved parties within the union. There has been a substantial escalation of violence across the delta oilfields, accompanied by major attacks on oil facilities. The problems of criminality, political disorder and insecurity now extend far beyond the geographical space of the Niger Delta, with militias causing mayhem in the western part of the country in a struggle over oil space.

The start of year 2016 saw the rise of a new group of militants called the Niger Delta Avengers (NDA) who claimed to be different to the earlier agitators and militants that operated under the umbrella of the Movement for the Emancipation of the Niger Delta (MEND) since 2005. By mid-2016, other groups such as the Isoko Liberation Movement, Adaka Boro Avengers and the Red Egbesu Water Lions joined the NDA in an alliance to wage war against oil installations, the government administration of Muhammadu Buhari and the Nigerian state as a whole. The groups were known to work in concert with the Indigenous People of Biafra

(IPOB), also a new militant group led by Nnamdi Kanu in the eastern part of Nigeria agitating for Biafran causes.

While it seems the name 'Niger Delta Avengers' is coined to serve as a thematic and definitive umbrella for renewed insurgency in the oil region, it also throws up the question of vengeance against who? Perhaps, vengeance directed towards the ex-president Dr. Goodluck Jonathan (a Niger Deltan himself) who ascended the presidential seat through what some call 'divine' arrangement to finally sort out the big Niger Delta problem. A task in which he failed, and woefully too. Recall that in 2009, late President Umaru Yar'Adua introduced an amnesty programme to end the Niger Delta insurgency. Two years earlier, ex-President Olusegun Obasanjo had deemed it necessary to allocate the Vice Presidency to the Niger Delta. By sheer providence, the occupier of this position, Goodluck Jonathan soon became Acting President following the death of Yar'Adua. Jonathan went on to win the presidential election in 2011 and became new president of Nigeria.

Roughly seven years into the amnesty programme introduced by Yar'Adua and sustained by Jonathan, Niger Delta militants were alleged to have been demobilised and disarmed. Insurgent leaders soon became security consultants to the Federal Government, monitoring pipelines, and assisting the government in tackling oil theft. The middle cadre was placed on monthly stipend while those that could be trained were sent to technical colleges and universities in foreign countries. In no time, the militants became rich and gentrified; and with their kinsman as President, the insurgents from the Niger Delta began to feel a sense of ownership and belongingness that has not been felt in the region since Nigerian independence in 1960.

Meanwhile, there were protests over the distribution of amnesty largesse, and disagreements among the former militants, who practically relocated to Abuja (the federal capital city) to take advantage of their brother's ascendancy to power. The quarrel was all about who got what, and it was only a matter of time before those who felt short-changed would stage their own drama, which they have now started in the hope that they might be luckier this time around and get their own share of appeasement. This is the sub-text of the deliberate distancing of the new boys from the old guard of militants, and the renewed criminality in the oil region.

Whether deemed an umbrella organization, a franchise or an un-united hydra; one thing that is certain is that the NDA emerged on the back of a long process of mobilising from below, widening social base, and institutional incorporation of various youth groups in complex and unstable networks. Consolidating a shift from non-violent protest, demonstrations, to occupations, sabotage, vandalisation to outright organised armed assault, and since 1998, the tactical use of kidnapping and ransom. Running across this story is the deepening involvement of the organised militias in various economic 'enterprises' including oil bunkering (and refining), extortion, protection services and drugs trade. Why has the 'Delta Farce' turned to 'Nigeria's Oil Mess'? Where did it all went wrong for the country?

****

Nigeria is the most populous country in Africa and the tenth largest country by population in the world. It is situated in the eastern terminus of the bulge of West Africa, on the Gulf of Guinea. It has an area of 923,768.00 square kilometres, and lies entirely within the tropical zone between latitude 40 and 140 north of the

14

equator, and longitudes 30 and 140 east of the Greenwich Meridian. The country's national boundaries are the result of its colonial history, a situation similar to most African countries. Nigeria is bounded on the east by the Federal Republic of Cameroon, on the west by the Republic of Benin, and on the north by the Republic of Niger. On the northeast is Lake Chad and on the south, the Nigerian coastline is bathed by the Atlantic Ocean. Its estimated population of over 150 million people represents twenty percent of the total African population, and constitutes a number of distinct ethnic groupings that vary from two hundred and fifty to as many as four hundred with language as the most widely used marker of ethnicity.

The recent history of Nigeria is embedded in the identity of Kingdom states based on ethnicity that has carried over into current day democratic Nigeria – the Yoruba, Edo, Igbo, Annang, Efik and Ibibio being prominent in the south, the Nupe in the middle belt and the Hausa, Fulani and Kanem-Bornu in the north. The King of Kanem embraced Islam in the eleventh century, about the same time that walled cities began to appear among the Hausa states taking advantage of their position along caravan route to engage in trade. The Oyo empire flourished in the southwest and the Benin Kingdom stretched as far as Onitsha. By the 18th century, Igalas and Igbo traders had settled in Onitsha.

Being a multi-ethnic and post-colonial state, a dominant feature of post-coloniality in Nigeria is the structural coexistence of and friction between the 'traditional' and 'modern' in the cultural, social, economic, legal and political frameworks of society. In contemporary African social anthropology, this phenomenon is termed 'structural dualism'. The structural dualism implies that the inherited colonial contradictions between communitarian and

15

capitalist economies, traditional and modern political systems, customary and common laws, are far from settled in the present dispensation and that, largely operated by indigenous actors, the Nigerian post-colonial state is confronted with new dialectics in the context of both 'old' (metropolitan forces) and 'new' (post-colonial elite) interests. This feature both portrays the unfinished nature of state-making in Nigeria, and compounds the institutional and instrumental constraints of the central authorities in unifying the disparate ethnic nationalities within the polity into a 'modern' nation-state.

In the above context, understanding the colonial character of the Nigerian state is a crucial factor in explaining its praetorian instincts in its oil producing region. In 1879, at the instigation of Sir George Taubman Goldie, all British commercial interests in the Niger area were channelled through the United African Company (UAC). The British bought out French interests on the lower Niger in 1884 thus clearing the way for British claims in West Africa to receive international recognition in 1885 at the Berlin conference. From 1885, the delta region of the Niger River became the British Oil Rivers Protectorate until 1893 when it was expanded and became the Niger Coast Protectorate. In July 1886, a charter was granted to the Royal Niger Company (RNC). Unfortunately, the RNC could not survive against the continued pressure from France and Germany. Thus, on 1st January 1900, RNC transferred its territories to the British Government where they were merged with the Niger Coast Protectorate to form Nigeria, a British protectorate and part of the British empire.

Even before it was officially incorporated into the British Empire in 1900, the Niger Delta had a long history of external commercial engagement. Early outside contact was primarily through the export of slaves. After the British banned the slave trade, palm oil became a key export commodity. The RNC dominated governance and trade, considerable hostility to its exploitative monopoly practices culminated in an attack on its Akassa headquarters by the King of Brass in 1895. A factor that led the RNC to sell its controlled territories to the British Government in 1900. The Niger Coast Protectorate was later incorporated into the Southern Protectorate, which was then amalgamated with Northern Protectorate in 1914 to form a unified Nigeria.

In the pre-colonial era, the Nigerian economy was traditionally based on agriculture and trade. This changed profoundly under colonial rule as the British colonialists transformed the commercial sphere of influence inherited from the RNC into a viable territorial unit under effective British political control. The British colonial economic policy was not to create a stable country but to promote a successful colonial trading station for the benefit of the colonialists. From the revenue generated through agriculture and taxation of farmers were intense public works such as harbour dredging, road and railroad construction in order to open the country to economic development. The British soap and cosmetics manufacturers took advantage of this infrastructural improvements in Nigeria by aiding the exploitation of the primary resources that were needed in British industries in the 'motherland'.

Just as colonialism impacted on the development in Nigeria from 1893 to 1960, the year Nigeria gained independence from Britain, the Transnational Oil Corporations (TNOCs) perpetuated in the Niger Delta oil region what the colonialists first started. The Niger Delta area is famous for its enormous crude oil reserves. The present day Niger Delta region comprises of 9 states out of the 36 states plus the centrally located Federal Capital Territory of Abuja in Nigeria namely: Abia, Akwa-Ibom, Bayelsa, Cross River, Delta, Edo, Imo, Ondo and Rivers. It is an area measuring about 16,000 square miles and roughly the size of Scotland in the United Kingdom. This massive wetland renowned for its huge crude oil reserves covers an area of about 70,000 square kilometres spreading over coastal mangroves, freshwater swamp and lowland rain forests. It is interspersed with a web of creeks and lagoons that runs through the River Niger into the Atlantic Ocean at the Bight of Biafra.

During the rainy season with a high degree of rainfall, humidity is above 80 percent, and road travel becomes almost impossible. The river normally discharge due to the high level of rainfall, this combined with the flat terrain of the soil causes enormous erosion and flooding. The defining characteristics of the Niger Delta ecosystem is the seasonal flood, erosion and sediment deposition. By nature, the Niger Delta region has a peculiar challenge posed by its harsh environment, which has made infrastructural development a herculean task by successive government administrations in Nigeria.

Nonetheless, within the delta challenging terrain known as the 'Oil River' in the nineteenth century, is an estimated thirty million people known as the Niger Deltans. The Niger Deltans referred to as the oil minorities in this book are made up of over three thousand ethno-linguistic communities. The Ijaws that cut across the four states of Bayelsa, Delta, Ondo and Rivers remains the largest ethnic group in the region. The other ethnic groups comprises the Ibibio, Anang, Oron in Akwa Ibom State; Bekwarra, Efik, Ejagham in Cross River State; Isoko, Itsekiri, Urhobo, Igbo in Delta State; Edo,

Etsakos, Igbira, Okpameri in Edo State; Yoruba, Ilaje in Ondo State; Igbo in Abia and Imo States; Andoni, Ibani, Ekpeye, Engenni, Epie-Atissa, Nembe, Ogoni, Okrika, Ogba in Bayelsa and Rivers States.

The daily survival of the oil minorities is based on a mixture of subsistence farming, fishing and petty trading especially in palm oil. Despite the Niger Delta region providing Nigeria's total proven reserves of oil standing close to 37.2 billion barrels as of 2015, the indigenous people are one of the most impoverished people in the world. One explanation is because of the politics of exclusion inherent in the formula for revenue allocation in Nigeria - that is the way oil rent is shared between the different layers of government. While the state and its political elite do not participate in the actual production of oil, they allocate the rents and profits from oil sales. As such, who benefits depends on one's position or closeness to those at the top echelon of state power.

The deprivation of the local people has been further compounded by the oil production activities of TNOCs, with marine lives and species endangered in large numbers in the region's wetland. Toxic effluents from crude oil exploration and drilling mud are often dumped in rivers and farmlands across the region; hence, undermining the environmental security of the indigenous people. The ecological despoliation of the area has had a negative impact on the people's ability to survive by subsistence means. Oil spillage and the burning of excess natural gas extracted during oil pumping known as gas flaring has created poor atmospheric conditions and contamination in the oil producing region. The effect on health and agricultural activities has been unimaginable.

Despite all these, the average Niger Delta inhabitant has little opportunity to seek legal redress, because it can

19

be costly, lengthy and complicated. As a result, militancy becomes a means of agitating for environmental protection and greater resource control. In recent years, the militancy has evolved through different dynamics, with the one based on violence and the struggle for power the most potent. This has led to the struggle over oil space, with the state devising numerous conflict intervention and management approaches of which securitisation has been the most obvious. With securitisation, armed troops are deployed by the state to the oil region in Nigeria to prevent protests or violence by the oil communities. This strategy of conflict management by the state has often resulted to open confrontation and a cycle of violence that has further claimed innocent lives.

Chapter 2 –

The Tragedy of Endowment

Perhaps more than anywhere else in the world, the Niger Delta exemplifies the paradox of poor human and social development in an environment of riches. The region's abundant natural resources, especially its oil, offer a potential foundation for development and posterity. Instead, while providing Nigeria with most of its wealth, the delta remains underdeveloped and afflicted by conflict and violence. The web in the oil region has been difficult to untangle, but the key actors have been the leadership of the Nigerian state, oil producing communities and Transnational Oil Corporations (TNOCs). Although the preponderance of oil violence in the Niger Delta became pronounced in the last two decades, the roots of the problem date far back, such that most of the recent problems only feed on historical issues.

Crude oil was first discovered in the Niger Delta community of Oloibiri, a small, remote creek community near Yenagoa in present day Bayelsa State in 1956 by Shell BP Petroleum Development Corporation of Nigeria Limited, a joint venture between Shell and British Petroleum (BP). It wasn't until 1958 that the first barrels of Nigerian crude oil destined for the world market departed Port Harcourt harbour, to be precise on the 17th February 1958. To navigate its way through the shallows of Bonny River, the 18,000 ton tanker 'Hemifusus' left from the Port Harcourt dockside half full. A shuttle tanker accompanied the Hemifusus to Bonny Bar, eight miles from the coast, where another 9,000 tons was pumped into the hold. Since then, oil production and export have been carried out by Shell and other TNOCs in Nigeria.

When the first helicopters landed in Oloibiri in 1956 near St. Michael's Church to the astonishment of the local residents, few could have predicted what was to follow. A camp was quickly built for workers, prefabricated houses, electricity, water, and a new road followed. Shell BP (as it was known then) sunk seventeen more wells in Oloibiri, and the field came to yield over 20 million barrels of crude oil during its lifetime before operations came to a halt twenty years after the first discovery. Misery, scorched earth, and capped wellheads are all that remains. Shell BP quickly discovered another giant oilfield at Bomu in Ogoniland, west of Port Harcourt in present day Rivers State in 1958. By now Shell BP has acquired fourty six oil mining leases covering 15,000 square miles across the oil basin.

In the decade that followed, the Bonny Tanker Terminal was opened in April 1961. The extension of the pipeline system which included the completion of the Trans Niger Pipeline was concluded in 1965 connecting the oilfields in the western Delta near Ughelli to the Bonny Export Terminal; and twelve giant oilfields came on stream including the first offshore discovery at Okan near Escravos in 1964. Oil tankers lined the Cawthorne Channel like participants in a local boat race, plying the same waterways that in the distant past, housed slave ships and palm oil hulks. By 1967, three hundred miles of pipelines had been constructed and 1.5 million feet of wells sunk, output had ballooned to 275,000 barrels per day (bpd). For the first decade of commercial extraction

(1958-1968), the foreign oil companies controlled the entire equity, production, export and marketing of Nigerian oil. They merely paid royalties and taxes to the Nigerian government. The Nigerian government largely basking in the euphoria of political independence was apparently contented with the significant monetary gains it derived in rents from the oil business, without having to make any tangible investments. As a result, Nigeria became labelled a 'rentier state' because of its oil dependent political economy.

Likewise, the country has been referred to as a 'petro state' because of the federal government's strong hold on the country's oil wealth. Within the Nigerian petro state is a degree of 'oil complex' due to the different actors and interests involved in the extraction and production of oil. This structure surrounding the political economy of Nigerian oil include the state, TNOCs, private and state security apparatuses, and external military interest in regional oil. During this post-colonial phase, government regulation and supervision of TNOCs' activities has been quite negligible. The TNOCs soon grew quickly in scale and complexity.

For the oil minorities (Niger Deltans), the large oil earnings were expected to be the dawn of a new era of rapid and sustained improvement in the living standards and overall wellbeing of the population. One that will support a self-reliant and dynamic economy based on a just and egalitarian society. How wrong were they? Authoritarian rule in form of military governance and the use of the state instrument of violence (armed forces) to pursue the interest of the custodian of state power, exacerbated the development plight of the Niger Delta. The gradual reductions in the derivation component of revenue allocation between 1960 and 1984 from 50 percent to 1.5 percent, the proliferation of states and local government areas, and the introduction of other criteria of revenue allocation such as need, population, and equality of states denied the Niger Delta area adequate funds for development.

This sense of exploitation and injustice, occasioned by what some oil minorities described as 'internal colonialism' arrangement, was aggravated by the fact that decisions to centralise oil resources were taken and imposed by federal military regimes (and their elected successors) representing dominant social forces. Since oil resources were mostly found in the Niger Delta, which is occupied by minority ethnic groups, the change in the revenue allocation formula was perceived by the oil minorities as a ploy orchestrated by three major Nigerian ethnic groups namely the Hausa-Fulani, Yoruba and Igbo to exploit them. The centralist nation-building project of the military in post-civil war Nigeria, bankrolled with petro-dollars, manifested as a virtual transfer of oil wealth from the Niger Delta to other regions of the country. The very process of national development paradoxically contributed to Niger Delta underdevelopment as the region, which generated oil that fuelled development, continued to lack basic amenities and infrastructure. Moreover, there were no links between the contribution of the region to the public till and its representation in the federal government, bureaucracy and public agencies. The marginalisation of the region and the progressive degradation of the environment due to oil exploitation and impoverishment, increased the minorities' feelings of frustration against the federal government and TNOCs, and provided the context within which protests and popular agitations transformed from one phase to another.

****

The first major episode of violent insurgency in the Niger Delta occurred in February 1966, on the eve of the succession of the Eastern Region, or Biafra, which included the eastern oil producing delta. Isaac Adaka Boro, an Ijaw born in Oloibiri and leader of the Niger Delta Volunteer Force (NDVF), declared independence of the Niger Delta People's Republic, consisting of the present day Rivers and Bayelsa States. Boro's abortive twelve-day revolt anticipated the Biafra civil war, as both conflicts were motivated by the control of oil revenue. Boro called for TNOCs to negotiate directly with his government rather than with the national authorities. Over a year later in May 1967, the Eastern Region of Nigeria renamed itself the Republic of Biafra, plunging the country into civil war. In the same month, the federal government broke the East into three states. One was Rivers State, which included many of the minority groups of the delta, as well as the bulk of the oil producing areas. However, any expectation of greater resource control was disappointed, as the federal military government transferred the control of oil resources to itself through legislation both during and after the civil war. The 1969 Petroleum Decree gave the federal government ownership and control of all petroleum resources in the country. In 1978, the Land Use Decree nationalised all land under the administration of state and local governments.

The centralisation of resources reduced tensions between the dominant ethnic groups of the federation namely the Hausa-Fulani, Yoruba and the Igbo. At the same time, exacerbated tensions between these large groups and the oil minorities in the Niger Delta, who became increasingly marginalised from the political and economic systems. As a result, the Nigerian oil region became a monument to

25

an exploit-and-abandon culture, and a poster child for the fairy tale of oil. That which inspires people to devote their lives to social change is sometimes an accumulation of experiences and knowledge, slowly building into an articulate conviction. It may be when resistance takes new forms, that an entry point becomes obvious. Other times it comes like a bolt of lightning, a sudden shift after a single event such as an arrest, the destruction of a beloved place, a conversation or the death of a loved one. This was no different in the case of the Niger Delta as the functions and mode of operation of militias in the delta region began to change in the mid-1990s, because of the new challenge of how to secure power and the right to have a greater say in the way the land and its natural oil resources were utilised. The economic and political marginalisation of the oil rich Niger Delta communities led to the radicalisation of its youths and brought about the idea of insurgency as a way of overcoming the injustice perpetrated by the state political elite and the TNOCs.

Although, certain observers through the 'greed' rather than 'grievance' analysis have questioned the above premise, arguing that it is the greed and self-enrichment motives of the militias that has served as a motivation for the oil conflict. While the greed argument carry some weight, given that former Niger Delta insurgent leaders later became either corporate or government contractors or politicians, the complicity of the Nigerian political/petro-elite and TNOCs cannot be underestimated when analysing the instability and human insecurity in Nigeria's oil delta. To the author, the context of the Nigerian form of petro-capitalism (or oil complex) created the economic motivation for militancy that later degenerated to full blown insurgency in the region. Therefore, it could be argued that the inequalities of petro-capitalism that engages with the "grievance rather than greed" analysis is best suited to explain the rise of insurgency in the Niger Delta.

The following three distinct phases are observed in the evolution of insurgency in the Niger Delta region of Nigeria:

i. the development of militias until 1998. This period coincides with the struggles for environmental and human rights in the Niger Delta region with the birth of the Movement for the Survival of Ogoni People (MOSOP) as its focal point;

ii. the phase between 1999-2007, when militancy took the form of full blown insurgency. This period coincides with the transition from military to civilian regime in 1999 where aside the oil related security issues in the Niger Delta, militias were used by the political elite to suppress opposing political candidates and their supporters in a violent political game that involved the supply and use of sophisticated weapons;

iii. the phase from 2007-2016, a period successive Nigerian governments has dubbed the 'era of domestic terrorism' in Nigeria. This period marks the beginning of bomb detonation as a way of registering grievance against the state in Nigeria by Movement for the Emancipation of the Niger Delta (MEND). An umbrella organisation for several militia groups in the Niger Delta, which was formed in 2005 to actively challenge the Nigerian state and its security apparatus. The group disrupts oil operations and kidnaps oil workers, most especially expatriates as a form of resistance. MEND also use public relations as a means of airing its demands.

Chapter 3 –

A Turbulent History

Of all the oil conflicts witnessed in recent years, the Niger Delta's case shows a complex mix of power and politics. It highlights the interface between local claims and the politics of international control in Nigeria's oil region. As accounted earlier, in 1966, exactly six years after Nigeria gained independence, an ethnic Ijaw policeman named Isaac Jasper Adaka Boro led the first rebellion for self-determination in the Niger Delta against the Nigerian state. In what observers hailed a mini-revolution, Isaac Boro assembled a group of Ijaw men to fight for the independence of the Niger Delta region from the Nigerian state. On 23rd February 1966, Boro raised the flag of a 'Niger Delta People's Republic' and declared previous oil contracts and agreements between the Nigerian state and the Transnational Oil Corporations (TNOCs) as null and void. Sadly, within twelve days of this rebellion, Boro was subdued by the might of the Nigerian armed forces. Today, Isaac Boro is regarded as a national hero within the Ijaw nation for his bold attempt to liberate his people from the whims and caprices of a repressive state.

With the economic decline of the 1980s came the upsurge of Niger Delta civil society groups whose aims were to publicise and seek redress for the economic and environmental grievances of the people. The politics of resource governance in the region assumed another dimension during this time. Groups such as the Niger Delta Human and Environmental Rescue Organisation (ND-HERO), Ijaw National Congress (INC), Ijaw Youth Council (IYC), Movement for the Survival of Ogoni People (MOSOP), Isoko National Youth Movement (INYM), Concerned Youths of Oil Producing States (CYOPS), Niger Delta Peace Project Committee (NDPPC) and so on, developed armed wings in the late 1980s and 1990s as ethnic militias or informal security groups. The groups, based on ethnic affiliations, were exclusive of each other, even though, they tried to address common political, economic and environmental woes.

As the economic marginalisation in the Niger Delta region worsened, coupled with the high record level of youth unemployment, the youths in anger and frustration looked for outlets to vent their emotions. Strengthened by the ideology already adopted, one in which they saw themselves as a repressed people, the young militias started agitating against TNOCs. By the late 1980s, oil theft commonly referred to as 'oil bunkering' became well pronounced and rose steadily throughout the subsequent years. Oil pipelines were vandalised by angry youths and members of militia groups, profits were also made from the sale of stolen oil.

Subsequently, TNOCs began to seek security protection of their facilities from the Nigerian state as a joint venture partner, one which the state political elite willingly agreed to despite the prevailing circumstances. In order for the federal and state governments to maintain security for TNOCs against the perceived threats from the local communities, the Supernumerary Police and security guards were deployed to various oil facilities across the region. This aggravated the tension between the state and its citizens, and led to further direct confrontations between the Nigerian state, its TNOCs and the environmental and human rights movements in the Niger Delta.

In its 1999 report titled 'The Price of Oil', Human Rights Watch (HRW) gave a vivid account of the police operation sanctioned by the Nigerian state against the oil-producing community of Umuechem whose indigenes were staging a protest at the Shell's facility based in the community. According to the report, the incidence of 30th and 31st of October 1990 that led to the extrajudicial killing of eighty unarmed protesters and the destruction of 495 houses, remains the most serious indictment of state-corporate alliance in the Niger Delta oil conflict history.

The event started on the 29th of October 1990 when Umuechem youths through peaceful protest demanded from Shell the infrastructural development of their community. This called for the provision of drinkable water, electricity and roads, to serve as a form of compensation for the environmental pollution caused by Shell's exploration activities in the area. However, rather than listen to the grievances of the oil community, Shell's divisional manager in person of Udofia J.R. wrote a letter to the state Commissioner of Police in Rivers State requesting for a deployment of the renowned paramilitary Mobile Police (MOPOL) locally known as 'Kill and Go'. The security response that followed led to the loss of innocent lives that were supposed to be protected by the state.

The subsequent judicial commission of inquiry set up by the government exonerated the local people of posing any threat through the peaceful demonstration, while the police were accused of having "a reckless disregard for lives and property". Yet, the actual perpetrators of this heinous crime within the state security apparatus have never been brought to book nor have the victims or their relations ever been compensated. This poses the question of whose security is paramount when it comes to national security calculation in Nigeria? Is it that of the citizens or that of the global capital as represented by TNOCs? One thing is however clear, that the security assault and state repression in Umuechem led to further grievances among the Niger Delta inhabitants, which nurtured the cycle of violence that has endangered the Niger Delta and the Nigerian state ever since.

The most well-known and highly publicised of the activists' movements in the Niger Delta was MOSOP, a socio-ethnic movement pursuing civil and environmental rights. The movement was led by a younger generation of Niger Delta elite who had previously served in the state bureaucracy. The young elite were determined to re-negotiate the 'social contract' to reflect the current context of the political economy of the Niger Delta region. MOSOP fought for the minority rights of the Ogoni people in the Niger Delta. In the 'Ogoni Bill of Rights' presented to the Nigerian government in the year 1990, the Ogoni people demanded for:

a certain degree of political autonomy;

a fair proportion of Ogoni oil wealth towards its societal development;

adequate compensation for the degradation of its environment due to oil extractive operations of TNOCs; and

the setting up of a Sovereign National Conference by the Nigerian government, where all ethnic nationalities can renegotiate their continued membership of the Nigerian state on an equitable basis.

Through widely publicised rallies and demonstrations, MOSOP empowered the Ogoni people to claim their oil-rich environment, declaring that the struggle for self-determination was not only morally just but also right. The movement identified the Nigerian state and Shell as the major actors to be targeted, highlighting that the reward of a successful pursuit of their struggle will eventually outweigh the costs. By deriving its legitimacy from the mass support received in Ogoni communities and the entire Niger Delta region, MOSOP became the umbrella organisation for different interest groups in Ogoni land. Groups that comprised the: Council of Ogoni Churches (COC), Council of Ogoni Professionals (COP), Council of Ogoni Traditional Rulers (COTRA), Federation of Ogoni Women (FOWA), National Union of Ogoni Students (NUOS), National Youth Council of Ogoni People (NYCOP), Ogoni Teachers Union (OTU) and so on.

By 1992, MOSOP had successfully mobilised the local people in Ogoni land to wrest control of their oil-rich environment from the state-petro-business alliance. The Nigerian National Petroleum Corporation (NNPC) alongside Shell and Chevron, another US oil company that operates in the Niger Delta, were given thirty days ultimatum to meet a list of demands or have their oil operations interrupted. Among the demands were:

Environmental Impact Assessment Study of TNOCs' oil exploration activities in Ogoniland in the last thirty five years;

Social Impact Assessment of TNOCs' extractive operations in Ogoniland since 1958;

Provision of infrastructures such as general and specialist hospitals to examine the health of the local

people who have been exposed to gas flaring in the past thirty five years;
Electricity and pipe-borne water to all Ogoni communities;
Review and payment of rents for all land seized by TNOCs from Ogoni land owners from 1958; and
The resettlement of internally displaced people in Ogoniland to new accommodations.

At this point, the adoption of militancy as a strategy to seek environmental justice by MOSOP coincided with the new global agenda of 'human security'. One that favoured the promotion of human and environmental rights. MOSOP took advantage of this new security discourse to form an international platform for its advocacy, and in doing so, exposed what was unprecedentedly one of the greatest environmental injustice of all time. The new human security discourse gave the oil producing communities of Ogoniland the global lever to wage their struggle against the Nigerian state and its TNOCs.

MOSOP resistance gained an international audience through its linkage with the Unrepresented Nations and Peoples Organisation (UNPO) at the Hague, Netherlands in 1992, and its connections with other International Non-Governmental Organisations (INGOs) such as Amnesty International, Human Rights Watch Africa, Greenpeace, Friends of the Earth, Rainforest Action Network and so on. Specifically, in an addendum to the Ogoni Bill of Rights that it published in 1991 titled 'An Appeal to the International Community', MOSOP alleged that the Nigerian military government under General Ibrahim Babangida have been unwilling to grant them audience despite been presented with legitimate demands in the Ogoni Bill of Rights.

By presenting its case to an international audience through a discourse that described the Ogonis and the entire Niger Delta population as a people faced with possible genocide from the combined might of a repressive Nigerian state and its TNOCS, MOSOP was able to garner local and international support and force Shell out of Ogoniland in 1993. This act tendered the stage for a militarised mediation by the Nigerian political elite, which saw the Rivers State Internal Security Task Force (RSISTF) and other state regular armed security personnel drafted in to Ogoniland and its environs in what was later described as a "militarised environmental governance" by certain commentators.

Military operations were sanctioned by the state to suppress the activist movement and protect oil facilities. New laws were drafted to complement state militarised response to the conflict in the region. In 1993, the 'Treason and Treasonable Offences Decree' was enacted by the Nigerian federal government under General Ibrahim Babangida, which made the agitation for self-determination by any minority group a treasonable act punishable by death. A year later, the Rivers State government enacted the 'Special Tribunal (Offences Relating to Civil Disturbances) Edict, under the Civil Disturbances (Special Tribunal) Decree of 1987'. This edict approved the death penalty for anyone or group involved in ethnic or communal conflict.

MOSOP leaders were subsequently arrested, detained and released several times in the new security strategy of the Nigerian state that involved intimidation and terror. Demonstrations and protests by local people at oil facilities were crushed by state security apparatus as it

34

became evidently clear that the struggle for resource control by MOSOP was far from being over. In order to avoid further confrontation to its hegemonic and extractive power, the State-TNOCs business alliance resorted to a 'divide-and-rule' tactic by recruiting onto its side a faction of the Ogoni elite, who had personal grievances to settle with MOSOP leadership. By this time, Ken Saro-Wiwa (1941-1995) assumed the leadership of MOSOP as president, with Ledum Mitee as the deputy president after the resignation of the previous leadership from their positions.

Sadly, on 21st May 1994, four Ogoni elite members were murdered by a youth mob in Gokana, an Ogoni community. The mob described the traditional elite members as 'hawks' conniving with their oppressors (Nigerian state and TNOCs) against their own kind. Ken Saro-Wiwa and other MOSOP leaders were arrested and charged for the murder of the four Ogoni elite under the Civil Disturbances (Special Tribunal) Decree of 1987. In the days that followed the escalating tensions, several Ogoni communities were ransacked and militarised through a strategy of securitisation. Independent accounts pinpointed indigenes most especially women and children as those that were mainly injured or/and displaced, with rough estimates putting the total loss of lives at about a thousand.

Despite international campaign for the Nigerian military government to drop the charges against the MOSOP leaders and respect the human rights of the Ogoni people, nine MOSOP leaders including its president, Ken Saro-Wiwa were executed by hanging on 10th November 1995. The global condemnation that followed the execution of the 'Ogoni Nine' led to the adoption of a resolution condemning the killings by the United Nations (UN)

General Assembly, and subsequently leading to the suspension of Nigeria from the Commonwealth. A fact-finding mission by the UN in Nigeria during March/April 1996 concluded that the trial of Ken Saro-Wiwa and the eight MOSOP leaders was flawed and illegal, because the Special Tribunal that held the case lacked the jurisdiction to try the accused.

Nevertheless, the suppression of the Ogoni activists and the securitisation of the region led to further development of militia movements such as the Chikoko Movement, Ijaw Youth Council and the Niger Delta People's Volunteer Force (NDPVF) that later became a formidable insurgent group in the region. Like in Umuechem and Ogoniland, other state military operations in the Niger Delta area defied all democratic and moral standards, offered a short-term national peace and security, as the resistance that followed state repression nurtured the cycle of violence that has since endangered the lives of the people. Such was the subsequent case in Kaiama in 1998/9.

Following the Umuechem and Ogoni crises and the subsequent demise of General Sanni Abacha, the military dictator that sanctioned the execution of Ken Saro-Wiwa and the eight Ogoni activists; the Ijaw youths met in Kaiama, Bayelsa State on 11th December 1998 to form the Ijaw Youth Council (IYC). The council adopted a declaration stating that the political crisis in Nigeria is an outcome of the "struggle for the control of oil mineral resources", and that the "degradation of the environment of Ijawland by the TNOCs and state arise mainly because Ijaw people have been robbed of their natural rights to ownership and control of their land and resources".

As a result, the IYC declared that it will no longer identify with any decree passed by the state without its participation or consent, and called for a stop to the militarisation of the region. Article 3 of Kaiama Declaration specifically states that:

"We demand the immediate withdrawal from Ijawland of all military forces of occupation and repression by the Nigerian state. Any oil company that employs the services of the armed forces of the Nigerian state to 'protect' its operations will be viewed as an enemy of the Ijaw people. Family members of military personnel stationed in Ijawland should appeal to their people to leave the Ijaw area alone".

The determination of the Ijaw ethnic group was further captured under Article 4 of the Declaration that stated:

"...demand that all oil companies stop all exploration and exploitation activities in the Ijaw area. We are tired of gas flaring, oil spillages, blowouts and being labelled saboteurs and terrorists. It is a case of preparing the noose for our hanging. We reject this labelling. Hence, we advise all oil companies staff and contractors to withdraw from Ijaw territories by the 30th December 1998 pending resolution of the issue of resource ownership and control in the Ijaw area of the Niger Delta".

On the contrary, on the 30th December 1998 while the Ijaw youths were demonstrating across Ijaw communities in support of the IYC Declaration, the state responded in a similar way to how it responded in Umuechem and Ogoni; and unleashed its coercive power on the youths. The Human Rights Watch report 'The Price of Oil' (1999) described the incident as a 'New Year Crackdown' that claimed dozens of lives of youths and three soldiers. In the days preceding the assault, truckloads of about 15,000 troops and two warships were reported to have been sighted by locals. There were eyewitness accounts of the heavy-handed response of the state's special paramilitary anti-crime unit codenamed 'Operation Salvage' created in August 1997 in Bayelsa State to protect oil facilities. The head of the paramilitary unit, Major Oputa, was reported to have commanded his troop to open fire on unarmed protesters in Yenagoa, the state capital. The violence and counter violence that followed the military intervention led to the declaration of a state-of-emergency by Lieutenant Colonel Paul Obi, the state military administrator. Lt. Col. Paul Obi had to ban all forms of meetings to avoid further violence.

Though the state-of-emergency was lifted on the 4th January 1999, the exact death toll of the military operation that lasted several days across Ijaw communities and the state capital has never been accounted for. The Human Rights Watch (1999) report suggest over 200 citizens were murdered by the state security apparatus across Kaiama, Yenagoa and other communities in Ijaw heartland. One thing certain from the event is that the military operation in Kaiama like the ones in Umuechem and Ogoniland, offered short-term national peace and security as the resistance that followed the state repression continued to nurture the cycle of violence that has endangered the lives of the Niger Delta inhabitants and Nigeria's national security.

After the events, attempts by the Nigerian state political elite and Shell to refine its image through global public relations campaign proved unsuccessful, because of the state's securitisation approach which had fuelled the locals especially the jobless and powerless youths into further resistance. These politically and economically disenfranchised youths in the Niger Delta had increasingly grown frustrated with the global-state oil alliance within the Nigerian oil complex, because of evident neglect, inequities and atrocities in the oil producing region. By 1998, the ethnic militias in the Niger Delta area were well established to challenge the Nigerian state and its political elite in a period of transition from military to civilian regime. While the militias were willing to be used as private armies by the political elite contesting for political offices and at the same time fight for a share of the limited resources available to them, the Nigerian state could no longer curtail the revolutionary pressures originating from the Niger Delta area of its territory.

****

The year 1999 marked a turning point in Nigeria's political history because it signified the handing over of political authority from the military to a civilian regime. During this time, the issue of environmental and national security had become a complex one with different ethnic groups and communal cleavages springing up in the Niger Delta. Militias were being recruited as political actors by local political elite to serve as ethnic paramilitary groups, but rather than being labelled as such, the militias were tagged 'political thugs' or 'opportunists' by the political elite and more recently by the local people of the Niger Delta. With unfettered access to sophisticated weapons made available to them by their political sponsors, the Niger Delta militias became more lethal and thus, expanded their scope of operation.

The struggle for environmental and economic resources became usurped by ethnic in-fighting as a result of the political competition among the Nigerian political elite. Evidence from the 1999 and 2003 national elections highlighted how hundreds of lives were lost and an estimated thousands displaced in the Niger Delta coastal communities of the Ilajes, Ijaws, Itsekhiris and Urhobos, because of ethnic militias in-fighting and rebellions against state security apparatus over political matters. In certain cases, federal troops were sent as reinforcements to curtail the violence, some of whom were attacked or even murdered by the militias. Though the act of murder is totally abhorred in all modern societies through constitutional provisions, some observers had actually called for the political elite that recruited and armed the militias in order to maintain political influence to be held responsible for the atrocities committed by the militants. Arguing that the shift to criminal violence concurred with the ascendancy of militant youths as political proxies.

However, after the Nigeria 2003 national elections, the militias were left in the cold as their services were no longer required by politicians who had either achieved or failed to achieve their political aim. Meanwhile, the already armed militias and still marginalised youths went back to their initial endeavour of fighting for whatever economic opportunities still available to them in the Niger Delta communities. Their strategy included kidnapping of expatriate oil workers for ransom, interrupting oil flow through oil installations vandalisation and in some cases, a total shut-down of oil production facilities. Aside monetary ransom made from kidnappings, the militias resorted to oil bunkering to sustain their insurgent activities. The crude oil siphoned from oil pipelines were eventually sold to international buyers with huge profits made by the militias, while the Nigerian federal treasury bears the brunt of the economic loss. Rough estimates put the figure of stolen oil at 70,000 to 300,000 barrels per day, with Nigeria's huge oil output reduced by an estimate of 15% in 2005.

Despite the Nigerian government militarised approach to curtail the rise of insurgency in the Niger Delta at the time, the forces of local resistance had intensified their struggle to challenge the authority and legitimacy of the Nigerian governing elite. In the fullness of time, crime became part of the resistance due to limited or non-economic opportunities for the jobless youths as some militias started operating for self-serving purposes.

By 2005, the Niger Delta insurgent groups have learnt from experiences of the past, especially from that of MOSOP. As a result, they devised new strategies of local resistance and global networking to support their cause. Attempts were made to upgrade the low intensity conflict in the delta region into a pan-Delta struggle for self-determination with the formation of Movement for the Emancipation of the Niger Delta (MEND). In its new strategies, MEND under the leadership of Asari-Dokubo adopted public relations through media awareness as a tool for fighting its cause by using a spokesman to communicate the group's intentions prior to carrying out any threat. With a vast amount of weaponry and firepower available to the group, MEND carried out debilitating attacks on oil installations and the Nigerian federal troops. The new violent methods were described as 'new war' by analysts due to the level of abuses and criminality involved.

On 1st October 2010 at Nigeria's 50th independence anniversary celebration in the federal capital city of Abuja, MEND successfully carried out a bomb attack in the city. The entire world at this stage realised how existential a threat the Niger Delta issue has become to the Nigerian state, with analysts and social commentators ascribing the event to 'the birth of domestic terrorism in Nigeria'. Could this incident have been avoided if an effective conflict management approach was put in place by the state and its political elite? In years that followed, other insurgent groups such as Boko Haram adopted similar strategies of bombing strategic locations and government facilities as a way of making their grievances known. A security issue that started in the swamps of the Niger Delta, has now impacted on the national security of the entire state.

****

Since 1999, few changes have been made to the government's construction of security strategies in the Niger Delta region. This is partly due to the continued military garrisoning of the oil region by successive government to checkmate further agitations and clamour for resource control. The struggle for an expanded access to resource wealth has been temporarily curtailed under an overwhelming military strategy and a contrived political amnesty programme by the state. There appears to be a continual shift towards securitisation as a way of suppressing the insurgency, other than just through military intervention.

For clarification, militarisation can be an aspect of securitisation, however, the distinguishing element is the rhetoric or discourse that often permeate the securitising act itself. State political elite are sometimes politically constrained to act arbitrarily or incautiously, therefore have to elevate certain political issues to the security realm in order to justify the action or response taken. In the case of Nigeria post-1999, the need to reflect a democratic image of the new civilian dispensation made state political elite adopt a subtle change of approach of first labelling the oil protesters and militants as 'criminals and terrorists', before taking military actions. Certain analysts contend that it was the post-9/11 Global War on Terror (GWOT) that made the subtle difference a desirable option for the Nigerian political elite, because of the fact that the international audience would readily buy into it. Hence, the significance in the merger between the Niger Delta security issues and the global security agenda.

Prior to the 1999 transition to democratic dispensation in Nigeria, the state have always been direct and swift in deploying military troops to areas where the free flow of oil was interrupted in the Niger Delta. Any minor conflict situation between host communities and TNOCs were met with swift government military responses. The periods between 1985-1998 under the military regimes of Babangida, Abacha and Abubakar saw massive military operations in the Niger Delta, whereby state security forces were used in combined operations with TNOCs private security to quell anti-oil protests resulting in heavy loss of lives. Ex-President Abubakar was quoted saying *"the state military authority would not permit any form of anarchy to be perpetuated in the Niger Delta area by its youth associations"*. Into the 1999 era of the new civilian regime of retired General Olusegun Obasanjo, little changed in terms of the government security tactics, except for the way the security strategies were constructed and sold to the wider audience.

In 1999, the Obasanjo civilian regime tried to open political dialogue with a selection of insurgent groups from the Niger Delta, this was seen as a ploy by the president to open up political space for his new administration. Given that the use of state instrument of force - military personnel, national police and so on to crackdown on insurgents in the course of protecting TNOCs' activities in the region continued unabated. A classic case is the Odi massacre in November 1999. Odi is a community endowed with crude oil in present day Bayelsa State in the Niger Delta. The community ordeal with the Nigerian state began when an alleged criminal gang operating out of Odi community headed by Ken

Niweigha, ambushed and murdered seven policemen who were on investigative duty in the area. Their actions prompted the president, Olusegun Obasanjo to issue an ultimatum to the state governor Diepreye Alamieyesigha, to either fish out the criminals within fourteen days or face the wrath of the state. However, before the ultimatum expired, the Nigerian army at the president's order stormed Odi community in a military operation code named 'Operation Hakuri II' led by Lieutenant Colonel Agbabiaka. The military operation led to the total annihilation of the town. According to the Human Rights Watch report 'The Niger Delta: No Democratic Dividend' published in 2002:

"the troops occupied the town for around ten days, and demolished every single building, barring the bank, the Anglican church and health clinic, and left graffiti that included ethnic slurs and reflected views that the town and the whole Ijaw ethnic group must be punished for the crimes committed by their sons".

Some of the graffiti left by the rampaging soldiers according to eyewitness accounts included slogans such as: we will kill all Ijaws; Bayelsa will be silent forever; nobody can save you; we were sent by government to kill and burn your community, take heart; we go kill all Ijaw people with our gun; Federal Government say No to Odi; the wicked shall not go unpunished; Odi where is your pride; come take the oil now. Foolish people; we don finish Odi. We don finish the work; and it came to pass; the end; Hakuri! Hakuri!

The final outcome of the raid was the total demolition of Odi town and its inhabitants. When questioned about the operation, Femi Fani-Kayode the Presidential Spokesman said:

"When we need to be hard, we have been very hard. We were very tough when it came to a place called Odi town where our policemen and our people were killed by these ethnic militants. And the federal government went in and literally levelled the whole place. And the proof of the pudding is in the eating. It has never happened again since that time. So I think that policy works".

He later went on to say that the operation was a:

"successful model of intervention that was aimed at criminal elements".

But with an estimated 2,483 people killed and the annihilation of an entire town, the questions asked was why would any government use such excessive force and endanger the lives of so many innocent citizens of Nigeria for the sake of arresting a handful of criminals? It makes no sense. Similarly, the National Assembly (federal parliament) delegate, under the leadership of late senate president Chuba Okadigbo, sent to inspect the scene described it as *"killing an ant with a sledge hammer".* Analysts have ranked the incident as the third biggest military intervention in Nigeria after the Biafra civil war and the 1990s genocidal attack on the Ogonis by the then military administrations. Yet, defending the government, Doyin Okupe the then Special Adviser to the president on media and publicity issued a statement saying:

"I wish to make it categorically clear that government, by this act, has not violated any internationally acceptable human rights provisions as practiced elsewhere in the developed world.... How can it be said that a carefully planned and cautiously executed exercise to rid the society of these criminals is a violation of human rights?"

The Odi attack happened under a civilian dispensation. It was interesting to note the contradictions emanating from different statements of government officials and representatives when questioned about the military operation in Odi. For instance, the then Nigerian Defence Minister retired General Theophilus Danjuma, while clarifying to an ECOWAS Ministerial Committee during a meeting held on 25th November 1999 stated that:

"This Operation Hakuri II was initiated with the mandate of protecting lives and property – particularly oil platforms, flow stations, operating rig terminals and pipelines, refineries and power installations in the Niger Delta".

General Danjuma's statement contradicts the earlier assertions of Femi Fani-Kayode the presidential spokesman, that the military operation was conceived to flush out criminal elements that waylaid and killed policemen who were investigating an alleged report of Ijaw youths invading Lagos. Therefore, Operation Hakuri II brings to light a number of questions that are yet to be answered by the state political elite. Questions like: was the military operation an attempt by the state to demonstrate it will not condone any challenge to its authority and rentier interests in the Niger Delta? Or was it just a case of the state maintaining national security by maiming and killing the very citizens that it was meant to protect?

Similar to the Odi military assault, were other cases in the Niger Delta where the political elite had unleashed state coercive forces on the oil producing communities, all in the name of fishing out criminals and terrorists. The military operations in Egbema (2004), Odioma (2005), Okerenkoko (2006), Gbaramatu Kingdom (2009) and Ayankoromo (2011) were specifically referred to as acts of state terrorism by some observers. These attacks were conducted under the military Joint Task Force (JTF) and were assigned different codenames like 'Operation Flush', 'Operation Fire-For-Fire', 'Operation Hakuri', 'Operation Strike Force', 'Operation Restore Hope', 'Operation Sweep', 'Operation Pulo Shield', and 'Operation Delta Safe' which is the most recent.

Obasanjo placed a blanket ban on all forms of militia activities the month following the Odi crackdown in December 1999, despite widespread condemnation of the security operation. This was similar to the decree imposed by Babangida against 'autonomous-seeking movements' in 1993, except that Obasanjo's was a specific target against individuals and youths involved in local resistance. The banning move by Obasanjo was seen as the beginning of a systematic criminalisation of the Niger Delta youths by the Nigerian political elite in order to justify future repressive acts in the region.

Furthermore, the outlawing of militias who once served as government approved vigilante groups to complement the police effort in the fight against criminality, was seen by some as a deft securitising move by the state political elite to reign in the militant youths. It is important to point out that it was not until the year 2002 that the state was able to ratify the ban, which eventually got ratified through the 'Prohibition of Certain Associations Act'. An act that bans associations or individuals or quasi-military groups formed for ethnic, cultural or social purposes or interests. This came on the heels of the new global war on terror as a result of the 9/11 terrorist attacks in the USA.

The new strategy of criminalising and terrorising the Niger Delta youths seem to pay off for the Obasanjo administration, as the government was able to deploy even more troops to the Niger Delta conflict areas. In August 2003, a new military JTF codenamed 'Operation Restore Hope' was created with 4000 Army, Naval and Air Force personnel to patrol the entire region of the Niger Delta. With modern helicopters and gunboats sometimes provided by external actors and TNOCs, the mandate of the military unit was to curtail oil theft and protect oil facilities and personnel, even though evidence suggest they often went beyond this brief. The U.S. Navy provided maritime security to support and help curtail oil theft in the region, despite the fact that the act of oil bunkering had been in existence since the 1980s. Oil bunkering is a lucrative business that involved an array of elites that cut across the political, military, economic, professional and traditional divide. However, as it is within the Nigerian oil complex, it is only the criminalised communities of the Niger Delta region that have borne the brunt.

The security situation in the delta region of Nigeria has continued to be tense and fragile despite the securitisation strategy of successive civilian administrations, and the political amnesty programme introduced in 2009. There has been a collapse of law and order in some oil producing communities, and the creeks and swamps of the Niger Delta have become ungoverned spaces due to the presence of militias. Evidence suggests that despite the presence of military troops in the delta region, formal governance structures have been largely undermined by the militias and protection rackets that trade security for cash. The resistance of the insurgent groups to continued marginalisation has led to further suppression and patronage politics on the part of the political elite, who are determined to protect their oil rents at whatever cost. This has been termed the 'politics of resistance and

48

accommodation' because of the complex nature of youth militancy and petro-capitalism.

The bombing, illegal trade in oil and kidnapping activities that started in the Niger Delta have become almost a daily occurrence in most parts of Nigeria. This has greatly undermined national security, compelling governments at both federal and state levels to allocate huge resources to security provision and maintenance. The insurgents genuinely believe that by threatening oil facilities which provided state revenues and profits to political elite and TNOCs, the government would be forced to accede to the demands of the ethnic minority people in the delta region. On the other hand, the state believe that by depicting the Niger Delta as a terrorist enclave, the youth militias can be eventually reined in. It is fair to say that such depiction suffers from improper threat analysis, as it overlooks the institutional context of the oil conflict. Instead of perceiving all militant activities as criminal and greed inspired, the interplay of all the sociological forces within the oil complex (elite, militants, TNOCs and civil society movements) should be considered alongside why they struggle for the control of oil space in the first place. If this is seriously considered based upon the realities of petro-capitalism, then the elite-(in)security nexus within the context of the Nigerian oil conflict could be better understood.

Chapter 4 –

The Rule of Oil

The evolution of the Nigerian political elite has been dictated by different circumstances of history. Over time, the elite has evolved and been able to overlap, converge and blend into a near perfect whole when it came to managing and allocating state resources; a situation that has rendered the elite less discernible even when the 'plural elite group' perspective is applied. According to Plural Elitism, power in modern democratic states is shared between a multiplicity of competing elites. A 'multiplicity of competing elites' that comprise of wealthy businessmen, senior administrators in both private and public sectors, seasoned politicians, professionals and traditional rulers, all of which represent main sources of power within the African context. Though in Nigeria, the process of elite formation and cohesion had been shaped by the British colonialists act of integrating the several ethnic groups and cultures into a single state.

There are five ethno-regional elite groups that sprang up in Nigeria towards the attainment of independence. These groups are the North, Yoruba, Igbo, Middle Belt and Niger Delta. The Northern elite also referred to as the Northern Oligarchy, originated from the northern part of Nigeria. It is dominated by the ruling elite of the Hausa, Fulani, Kanuri, and Nupe ethnic groups. The strength of these elite groups are drawn from a single religion and language, Islam and Hausa respectively. The

Yoruba elite originated from western Nigeria and comprise of sub-elite networks from the Yoruba towns of Ekiti, Ijebu, Lagos and Oyo. The Yoruba elite has the highest number of educated elite members in Nigeria owing to its early access to western education, which eventually helped in the nationalist struggle for independence. The Igbo elite originated from the eastern part of Nigeria, like the Yorubas, they had early access to western education that offered them administrative career opportunities.

The Middle Belt elite originated from the ethno-lingua minority groups, in what is today's north-central part of Nigeria. The people of this region have historically resisted the political domination of the northern Muslim Hausa-Fulani, and the religious domination of the northerners. The Niger Delta elite on the other hand, inspite originating from an ethnic and cultural heterogeneous region, share a similar history with the Middle Belt elite, one that has shaped its elite formation and political mobilisation. This elite group has historically been resisting an array of groups such as the British colonialists, the northern, Yoruba and Igbo elite groups, and the post-colonial Nigerian state. Under colonial administration, the Niger Delta was divided between the Western and Eastern regions for administrative ease. This delineation and colonial structure led to a 'master-servant' relationship between the inhabitants of the Niger Delta and the British colonialists, which later transformed to the Yoruba and Igbo dominance over the inhabitants of the Niger Delta in a post-colonial Nigeria.

In the 1950s, in the approach to Nigeria's independence, the oil minorities of the Niger Delta had argued over the British right to hand them over to the new nation-state, Nigeria. This argument was based on the desire of the local elite to maintain control over their

51

own affairs and the belief that a central Nigerian authority, most likely to be made up of non-Niger Delta ethnic groups, would seek to exploit the region's resources for their own betterment. However, the British response, stemming from Sir Henry Willink's Commission on Minority Groups, was to reject independence for the Niger Delta region, as well as granting it the status of a state within Nigeria. Though, the commission recognised in a foreshadowing of the complaints of today, that among the people of the Niger Delta lay a deep-rooted conviction which the authorities of the central government has failed to grasp. Therefore, it recommended the establishment of the Niger Delta Development Board (NDDB), which among other things, required that no less than 50 percent of the total revenues derived from the region be apportioned to it.

The complexities of the delta region became more convoluted in 1956 with the discovery of oil in Oloibiri. Little did anyone know that the future of the delta would take a dramatic and unexpected turn, with the discovery of oil by Shell BP at Oloibiri community. Like the 19th century palm oil boom that saw British colonial interests take hold of the Niger Delta, the discovery at Oloibiri meant that an independent Nigerian government would loath to loosen its control over the region. The rapid rise of oil revenues that was to dominate the Nigerian economy, had a reverse effect on the region from which the resources were being extracted. Much as it was feared, the oil minorities of the Niger Delta faced massive disenfranchisement by the larger ethnic groups, primarily by those at the helm of the Nigerian federal government. The people of the Niger Delta would only see poverty and environmental degradation from Nigeria's oil windfall.

The aforementioned inter-group lopsided arrangement partly led to the agitation for Niger Delta states by the oil minorities, even though others saw the subsequent struggle in the Niger Delta as a result of the oil economy. The present determination of the Niger Delta elite to seek further integration into the mainstream of Nigerian politics by using oil as a 'bargaining chip' might lend credence to this view. The paradox of the situation is in the level of mistrust not only seen between the northern and Niger Delta elite groups, because of the northern opposition to greater resource control; but also the amount of mistrust between the southern political elite, which include an all-inclusive Niger Delta elite, Yoruba elite and Igbo elite.

Unlike the pre-colonial traditional elite that were made up of Kings and chiefs, the different regional elite groups in colonial and post-colonial Nigeria were made up of individuals and their families that lived in Government Reserved Areas (GRA) and other working class neighbourhoods. Individuals aided by education, urbanisation, Westernisation and popular media, who led the struggle for independence and as such became nationalist leaders at independence. The elite and their followers later occupied influential positions of authority post-independence both at regional and federal levels, and became leaders of the major Nigerian political parties. Unfortunately, the prevalent politico-economic ideology of the 1960s that was centred on state-directed development allowed these regional elites either as politicians, civil servants or entrepreneurs, to capitalise on their positions and privately accumulate state resources; setting the process for elite domination in Nigeria.

****

The hitherto history of elite formation and evolution in colonial and post-colonial Nigeria has been the history of group contestation between different elite networks along ethno-regional fault lines. Political regimes post-independence has been observed from a democratic to authoritarian perspective, where regimes have either been civilian or military or at best a fusion of both. This has led to a simplistic and generic analysis of political elite's perception of threat and attitude towards national security by certain political scholars. In the attempt to provide insights into the constellation of the different forces within the Nigerian political spectrum, scholars have tagged the military elite as the bane of the Nigerian society.

The military elite who were perceived as the dominant elite group, has been held responsible for majority of the contradictions of the Nigerian society. Notwithstanding, the dominance of the military elite as true as it might be, has been over exaggerated to the point that the emergence of other elite groups such as the economic and professional in the Nigerian political scene tend to be overlooked. How powerful and influential these new groups have become in the area of policy-making in a recivilianised Nigeria has been understated.

This informed the argument in this book that political elite in Nigeria operates within exclusive networks that itself is predatory and disconnected from society. Similar background, recurrent appearances and vested interests are linked to elite practices such as repression, human rights abuse, patronage exchanges and corruption to enhance continuity in political offices. These cumulative practices and interests coalesce with inept state institutions to provide the dynamics for securing elite private interests and set back significant social change. Thus, continuity instead of renewal prevails in elite security practices with far-reaching negative effects on public security needs. The elite relies more on state power and institutions for survival than on the feedback from the Nigerian citizenry whose members clamour for elite responsiveness and protection.

****

The military intervened in Nigerian politics as a 'corrective regime' to right the wrongs of the first republic political elite. General Aguiyi Ironsi who became the military head of state after foiling the 15th January 1966 coup, introduced draconian acts to forestall opposition to the military regime. The authoritarian acts introduced included the abolition of political parties, parliament and interest groups. These were replaced with the Supreme Military Council (SMC), a political hierarchy established for state decision-making in addition to setting policy initiatives and agenda especially in the area of security. The ruling SMC usurped both executive and legislative powers while the judiciary were left at the caprices of the military elite. It is worth noting that military and civilian personnel were both appointed into the top echelon of government as advisers, even though few of these civilians were part of the inner circle of the ruling elite.

The structural changes made by General Ironsi provided insight into the strategy that subsequent military regimes will adopt in Nigeria. A strategy including an alliance of military and civilian personnel in governance, and the management of state resources. An alliance formed to wrest control of state power in order to further the particular interests of a selected few. Politicians, civil servants and businessmen capitalised on the new arrangement and connived with the military in power to set the process for elite domination and perpetuation in

55

power. Aside the diarchal arrangement, Ironsi created a unitary system of governance under the Unification Decree No 34 of 1966. Under the new unitary arrangement, the existing four regions: North, East, West and Mid-West, were made mere political units called 'provinces'. The timing of this power centralisation project, which included centralised resource control and weak autonomous units, was significant because right from the colonial days, whoever controlled state power also controlled the allocation of its resources. The control of state resources prior to this was regionally based because the regions were autonomous and relied on revenue from agricultural products for their development agenda. The revenue allocation principle was based on derivation whereby regions had 50% control over their resources.

The unfolding political context can be interpreted in one way. That the unification move was an attempt by the governing elite to protect their cronies' interest and their own personal aggrandisement. This is because the desire to accumulate wealth after this period led to increased elite competition for control of state resources and as a result, corruption became institutionalised among public office holders. General Ironsi was later toppled and killed in a counter coup. However, his centralist aspiration became the hallmark of the federal system that was later adopted in place of the unitary system of governance. Thus, Ironsi left an enduring paradox within the Nigerian political landscape.

On 29th July 1966, there was a counter coup by northern military officers who emerged as the new decision-makers within the military hierarchy. The counter coup led to the murder of many eastern military officers. Lieutenant Colonel Yakubu Gowon became the new Head-of-State. Gowon abolished the regional structure and in its place created twelve states. The abolition of regionalism impacted on Nigeria's federalism and its process of elite' evolvement and entrenchment. The peripheralised federal system was transformed into a centralised federation where the central government became much stronger at the detriment of the federating units. This shifted the competition for political power and resource control from the sub-national level (regions or states) to the national level.

The killings of easterners and Christians in the north further led to a mass exodus of easterners back to their ancestral Igboland in the eastern part of Nigeria. Chukwuemeka Ojukwu, a military governor of the eastern region and an Igbo-man, declared secession of the independent state of Biafra from the Nigerian federation. A move supported by countries like France, Portugal, and South Africa, but opposed by countries like the United Kingdom, United States and the Soviet Union, who supported the Nigerian federal government instead. Even though Gowon was able to conquer the Biafran secessionists through the military operation led by Olusegun Obasanjo, who later became both a military and civilian Head-of-State, Gowon's administration was best remembered for the high level of corruption resulting from the sales of crude oil and the enactment of Petroleum Decrees 9 and 51.

Decree 51 empowered the federal government to own, collect and allocate oil revenues, while issuing Oil Exploration Licences (OEL) and Oil Mining Licences (OML). Decree 9 extended the central government's rights of ownership to include oil revenues from offshore operations. Oil revenue rose steadily in the 1970s exceeding expectations, and corrupt military leaders both at federal and state level enriched themselves with state resources. The safeguarding of the state under the Gowon administration became costly in terms of governance, as the Nigerian Army rose from 10,000 member force to 250,000 with the military becoming a key and strategic political player.

Gowon re-established the Federal Executive Council (FEC) under a diarchic arrangement, whereby both military and civilian personnel were appointed to federal executive offices. The civilian personnel included permanent secretaries in the civil service and political advisers mostly made up of professionals who were entrusted with bureaucratic decision-making roles. Observers articulated that the military elite simply used the intellectual and bureaucratic elite to gain legitimacy, while in return the intellectuals and bureaucrats used their positions to take care of their own interests. A situation that has made the military-professional elites nexus difficult to analyse when it comes to who makes what decision and when during this time in Nigerian political history. Nevertheless, the appointments of the professionals was done to disguise the authoritarian nature of military regime to the outside world.

The appointed civilians who were co-opted to cabinet positions to give their expertise and perform administrative tasks tried to extend their scope of authority and influence by seeking avenues to gain further access to state resources. This was partly achieved through the enactment of the Nigerian Enterprises Promotion Decrees of 1972, an 'indigenisation' strategy that allowed foreign business concerns to be sold to indigenous people such as civil servants, businessmen and professionals that could afford them. While the option of local ownership was provided through this new economic nationalism, it was only the elite that had access to state resources such as the largely state-owned lending institutions that could afford to buy the equity in the foreign enterprises.

The emergent 'share-owning elite' were made up of upper level civil servants with better access to credit and information, leading Nigerian business executives with links to foreign companies, large scale businessmen and military officers who had acquired wealth in the 'quick-gain' sectors through contracting business. Thus, the indigenisation policy rather than being a policy of economic redistribution and local ownership, only enhanced the position of the new political elite while entrenching the socio-economic status quo. Consequently, the lines between the military, economic, intellectual, bureaucratic and socio-cultural elites became blurred as they all became stupendously rich and influential because of their access to state resources. Subsequent policies contrived by the military further contributed to the process of elite formation and consolidation in Nigeria. However, with a failing economy, unprecedented level of corruption and a federal government whose very own constituency (the military) had lost faith in its ability to move the nation forward both politically and economically, General Gowon was toppled on 29th July 1975 in a bloodless military coup by army officers of northern extraction. Brigadier Murtala Ramat Mohammed became the new Head-of-State and Commander-in-Chief of the armed forces.

Like Gowon, Murtala came from the northern part of Nigeria and put some structural changes in place on assumption of power. He reverted back to the old structure of governance introduced by Ironsi and partially adopted by Gowon where the SMC and FEC remained the national decision-making bodies. Though, the high civil servants were barred from attending decision-making meetings except on invitation. A new Council of States (COS) was formed comprising state military governors whose SMC membership had been previously withdrawn. These corrective institutional changes had a lasting effect on security decision-making in Nigeria (both under the military and civilian administrations), because state governors' assessment and input to security issues in their respective states became subservient to that of the federal authority. In addition, the intellectuals and bureaucrats who became powerful under the Gowon's administration, were curtailed and removed from the decision-making process.

The state of affairs reveals that even under military rule, there was a process of elite-recruitment that was taking place, as those who occupied the seats of political command were not fixed or permanent. The elite circulation through elite-recruitment process affected the form of governance during this era, even though it did not impact on the structure of military governance in Nigeria. The military elite at that point in Nigeria's national history, still remained the dominant elite group that influenced both political and security decisions.

Despite the infringement on the influence of civilian personnel in state decision-making, the Murtala administration set Nigeria on the path to democratic rule by inaugurating a constitution drafting committee that were charged with the responsibility of preparing a legal framework for the return to civil rule. Seven additional federated states were created within the seven months period that Murtala led Nigeria, increasing the number of states from twelve to nineteen to encourage grassroots politicking. However, the mantle of leadership fell on Murtala's deputy, Colonel (later Major General) Olusegun Obasanjo when on 13th February 1976, Murtala was murdered in an attempted coup led by Lieutenant Colonel B.S. Dimka. At his death, Murtala became another landmark figure in elite succession in the chequered political history of Nigeria.

Obasanjo is considered a key dominating political elite member in Nigeria. He was an army officer of southern origin in the north-south dichotomy of Nigeria. He was the army commander under the Gowon regime that led the final and heroic onslaught against the Biafran secessionists. He also endorsed and implemented the Nigerian Enterprise Promotion Decree enacted by Gowon through a review of the 'indigenisation policy' in 1977. The 'Land Use Decree of 1978' that placed ownership of all land in the hands of state and federal governments at the detriment of the real owners was the most significant act performed by his administration. The Land Act is a causal factor of the Niger Delta oil conflict. Obasanjo completed the transfer of power from military to civilian. Although, the new Nigeria national constitution was drafted by the military under his leadership, in place for the incoming civilian administration. By Obasanjo's side was a trusted and loyal deputy, Shehu Musa Yar'adua, an army officer from the north. Together they steered the affairs of Nigeria into the new civilian era under a period regarded as the second republic in Nigeria's political phraseology.

Alhaji Shehu Shagari of northern descent emerged as the second republic new civilian president of Nigeria in 1979 through a military sponsored election. A presidential constitution and system of government was adopted instead of the Westminster parliamentary system practised in the first republic. The change was driven by a general concern amongst the different elite ranks on the suitability of practising a parliamentary system in Nigeria, because of its complex social structures; hence, the need for an American styled 'executive president' to lead the various groups and nationalities in Nigeria. Consequently, the offices of the Head-of-State, Head-of-Government and Commander-in-Chief of the armed forces was merged into the presidency. This meant that the state including its armed forces fell under the authority of the civilian president.

The Shagari administration was characterised by violent politicking and endemic corruption. Political practices and decision making was based on convenience rather than on constitutional provisions. Offices were created to accommodate self-serving interests, and the entire machinery of government became bloated. Bribery, corruption and looting of public buildings to cover fraudulent acts became the hallmark of the Shagari administration. Despite all these, Shagari won a second mandate through a general election to lead the country for another four years term. A second leadership journey he embarked upon on 1st October 1983. However, on 31st December 1983, just three months into his second term, Shagari was overthrown by General Muhammadu Buhari in a bloodless military coup. Ending another landmark in the turbulent history of elite's succession in Nigerian political history.

Buhari, another army officer from the northern part of Nigeria, had less tolerance for the corrupt political elite. Together with his famous deputy, the late Brigadier Tunde Idiagbon, they initiated War Against Indiscipline (WAI), a corrective programme aimed at targeting the perceived negative social attitudes of Nigerians towards political authority. However, with a similar pattern inherent in previous military regimes, the Buhari administration suppressed the human rights of the civil populace by infringing on their freedom of speech. Through authoritarian rule, journalists were unfairly tried and jailed leading to friction in the civil-military relation. On 26th August 1985, Buhari's regime was toppled by Major General Ibrahim Babangida.

Babangida, who was Buhari's Chief of Army Staff and another officer of northern descent, was skilful in political craftsmanship. He appointed individuals from different segment of the society into his political bureau. The individuals were appointed to facilitate the transition back to democratic rule. To aid the transition, Babangida formed two political parties called the Social Democratic Party (SDP) and the National Republican Congress (NRC). The political parties' manifestoes were alleged to have been written by Babangida himself while at the same time instructing notable politicians on what party to join. His political reform alongside his economic reforms were implemented under a corrupt and repressive atmosphere. On 12th June 1993, a presidential election was held and a Yoruba businessman from the economic elite, and a mutual friend of Babangida in person of M.K.O Abiola, was alleged to have won the undeclared election. Babangida who was on course to leave office, annulled the widely acclaimed election and stepped aside for an interim national government, which he had set up. Thus, halting the 'third republic' in Nigerian political history before it had even began. Analysts have referred to it as a 'stillbirth' whose surgical operation was performed by the military elite.

During his rule, Babangida did initiate and implement bureaucratic reforms where 'career permanent secretaries' were made 'Directors General' of their different ministries or federal agencies. Insignificant as this might be, in principle, it meant these civilian personnel could be appointed and dismissed by the military authority. A situation that left them open to political manipulation and vulnerability. The caretaker civilian administration that was constituted after the annulment of the June 12 presidential election was headed by Ernest Shonekan, another member of the economic elite group and a close friend to Babangida. In November 1993, a High Court in Lagos State declared the interim government of Shonekan illegal. Shonekan's government was overthrown just a few weeks into his administration by General Sanni Abacha, the most senior military officer second to Babangida. Reports at the time suggested the court ruling was the perfect opportunity for Abacha to satisfy his long time ambition of becoming the president and Commander-in-Chief of the armed forces. Meanwhile, Abiola the acclaimed winner of the June 12th presidential election had been arrested and kept in custody by the Abacha military junta.

While Abacha had set up a constitutional conference to review the country's constitution, he ruled in an authoritarian military manner, quenching widespread anti-government protests by Abiola's supporters in southern Nigerian cities with brutal force. His coercive way of managing opposition and conflicts was extended towards the human rights community in Nigeria. Activists were either imprisoned or executed while in custody or out of prison. Such were the killing of Alfred Rewane, who was alleged to have been funding a pro-democracy group, National Democratic Coalition (NADECO) that was sympathetic to the June 12th election cause; and the state murder of Ken Saro-Wiwa in 1995, a Niger Delta activist and leader of the Movement for the Survival of Ogoni People (MOSOP). The Niger Delta oil conflict still remains a major security issue nationally, regionally and internationally. It is a conflict emanating from the struggle over environmental degradation, revenue allocation and resource control. It indicates the dysfunctional system in Nigeria where the political elite are more interested in the accumulation of state resources for their own interests rather than the national interest.

Former military Head-of-State now retired, Olusegun Obasanjo and his deputy, Shehu Musa Yar'adua were also imprisoned on alleged coup plotting activities against the Abacha administration. Shehu Yar'adua later died in custody. On 8th June 1998, Abacha died a natural death, ending one of the darkest episodes in Nigerian history and probably the most brutal of all the military regimes Nigeria has ever had. The following day (9th June 1998), another military officer from northern Nigeria named General Abdulsalam Abubakar took over the mantle of power as the new Head-of-State of Nigeria and Commander-in-Chief of the armed forces. Upon entering into office, Abubakar immediately set in motion the process for transition to democratic rule by granting amnesty to all political detainees including those that had fled the country; in doing so opening the political space for a broader political contest. Although Abubakar was seen to be committed to the democratic process, he was left with no choice given the fact that the military government had been shunned and condemned after the annulment of the June 12th election, and the murder of Ken Saro-Wiwa. There had also been international efforts to check the gross human rights violation perpetrated by the military elite in Nigeria. For instance, Nigeria was expelled from the Commonwealth of Nations while the High Commission of Canada in Lagos was closed and its ambassador recalled. The United States of America on its part downsized its U.S. Agency for International Development (USAID) mission in Nigeria.

By appointing a group of senior active duty and retired officers from the military establishment and businessmen from the economic elite group, Abubakar organised a transition government that ushered in the civilian 'Fourth Republic'. However, partly due to the fear that Nigerians might agitate for a new constitution, which they (the elite) might not be able to regulate or contribute to, Abubakar and his cohorts resuscitated the second and third republic Nigerian constitutions to protect officer-specific interests. The Peoples Democratic Party (PDP) was created as a national progressive party whose machinery will be used to end military rule on military terms. This brought about the selection of a former military Head-of-State, retired Major General Olusegun Obasanjo as its presidential candidate. Obasanjo, despite been imprisoned by Abacha, was part of the military elite in Nigeria. Being a Yoruba Christian from the south like M.K.O. Abiola, who was rubbed of the June 12th 1993 electoral mandate, he was seen as a perfect replacement.

Obasanjo won the controversial presidential election in 1999, which the election observation team sent by the National Democratic Institute, led by the former American president, Jimmy Carter, refused to endorse due to the massive nature of electoral fraud that happened. Notwithstanding, Obasanjo was sworn in on 29th May 1999, becoming the second executive president of a democratically elected government in Nigeria after Shagari. This period became known as the fourth republic in Nigeria's political parlance.

Obasanjo became the first president under the new 1999 constitution of Nigeria in the fourth republic. The constitution was similar to the 1979 version because it included provisions such as secular state, separation of powers, a bill of rights, federalism and multiparty system. The presidential system of government was readopted in the 1999 constitution. The cabinet referred to as the Federal Executive Council (FEC) became headed by the executive president. The vice president and other appointed ministers were answerable to the president. With its ascension to power, the Nigerian political elite headed by Obasanjo threw all democratic principles into the air and started behaving the same way as previous military administrations. The new political elite comprised men from the military establishment and civilians alike who had served under various military regimes. Within this elite group were bureaucrats and technocrats some referred to as professionals. The wielding of power by these political elite has been associated with corruption, diversion of state resources - oil rent and so on.

Over time, there was state-society as well as intra-institutional crises between the executive and the legislature resulting from tussles over resource allocation. Government stability was threatened because of oil pipelines vandalisation and kidnappings of foreign oil workers leading to disruption of oil production that affected revenue generation. Amid these security crises, Obasanjo tried to vie for a third term presidency, which was not provided for in the constitution, and failed. He eventually conducted elections having influenced the choice of presidential and vice-presidential candidates in the persons of president Umaru Musa Yar'adua and vice-president Goodluck Jonathan in 2007. Following which he relinquished power to his preferred candidates.

Umaru Musa Yar'adua was Shehu Musa Yar'adua's brother, who was Obasanjo's deputy during the military administration of 1976-1979. They were from a northern elite family of Fulani heritage in present day Katsina State. Umaru Yar'adua was Katsina State governor before being chosen to vie for the presidency by Obasanjo in 2007. The 2007 election that brought Yar'adua to power was described as one of the worst rigged election in Nigeria's history because of the massive irregularities that were reported. His political opponent was Muhammadu Buhari, the former military Head-of-State that overthrew the second republic civilian administration of Shagari through a military coup. Buhari disputed the election results and took his case to the law court but eventually lost. The point to highlight here is the calibre of individuals that keep re-emerging on the political scene both in government and in opposition. Individuals that have had some involvement with previous military administrations and therefore would share common background and probably similar interests which will influence their perception of security, or what constitute a security threat.

Umaru Yar'adua was not a man of sound health despite inheriting national insecurity from the previous administration. He passed away while on a medical trip and his deputy, Jonathan Goodluck stepped in as acting-president in 2009 during the trip and later as president in 2010 when Umaru Yar'adua passed away. In 2011, Goodluck Jonathan won the presidential election in Nigeria and became the third executive president after the 1999 military to civilian transformation. His rise was meteoric because he was a deputy governor in the Niger Delta state of Bayelsa until the then governor - late Diepreyie Alamieyesigha was controversially arrested in London due to money laundering allegations instigated by the Nigerian president - Obasanjo. Jonathan became the stand-in governor and held the position till he became the new vice-president in 2007 and later as president of the country till he handed power to Muhammadu Buhari, who contested against him and won in the 2015 general election.

Most of the political actors by early 2015 were still remnants of the same political class of 1999. The situation has been described as "recycling of the political gladiators". This was because successive Heads-of-State after Obasanjo until 2015 were his choice of candidates, and are meant to protect his interests and that of his cronies. A patron-client network pattern emerged at federal and state level of governance, because retired 'Generals' became the leading voices of their elite sub-groups. The other elite networks cling on to them for support, prompting an alliance that has been insidious for most part, and antithetical to political stability.

****

The analysis on the composition of the elite in Nigeria is to highlight the dominance of the Nigerian political elite. They initiate and supervise policies at the federal level of governance and assimilate all the other elite networks into their fold in order to influence power structuring at different levels of governance. The military's incursion to the body politic of Nigeria that began with the January and July 1966 coups paved the way for elite domination in Nigeria. It succeeded in removing the first republic political elite from power but failed to prevent the transformation of the forces produced by these military coups into becoming an evolving and dominating political force.

Contrary to the military's self-proclaimed objective of correcting the mistakes of the past, it became an agency for exacerbating them; which did not come as a surprise given the military's self-regulating mechanism that does not encourage feedback, and its monopoly of the means of violence. It was the military elite through its internal inter-ethnic rivalry that instigated the civil war (Biafra) and prosecuted it. The end of the civil war coincided with the substantial exploration of oil in the Niger Delta region of the country. The huge rent accruing from oil extraction referred to as 'oil bonanza' or 'national cake' in some quarters led to the centralisation of the economy and the emergence of a new political elite sometimes referred to as 'petro-elite'.

This transformative period threw up an alliance in which a coalition of high ranking military personnel, civil servants and representatives of local business concerns formed an alliance of military, civil service and big business to control state power, with the ultimate aim to influence and control access to the economic resources. This strategy of securing the positions of certain elite or private entrepreneurs had a profound effect on the Niger Delta oil conflict and governance in general, as it posits unequal distribution of rewards, private capital accumulation and socio-economic inequalities. Consequently, the social classes that emerged from these imbalances in the oil region have been dubbed 'the elite and the masses' or 'the wealthy and the poor' - perceptions that has contributed to further grievances among the inhabitants of the Niger Delta and Nigeria as a whole.

Chapter 5 –

The Big Heart - A Broken Heart

The Niger Delta dismal development narrative, especially the paradox implicit in the severity of the current development crisis, despite the large amount of foreign exchange earnings from oil exports raise a key question. The question of why has sustainable development been elusive in the Niger Delta region of Nigeria despite the magnitude of its oil wealth? It is incontestable that exploring, finding, producing, distributing, exporting and sharing the economic surplus from oil and gas exploitation encompass a multifaceted set of economic, social, political, environmental, engineering, scientific, strategic and legal issues that ought to be properly investigated. However, it is the belief and argument here that the Nigerian political elite as the custodian of the oil wealth, should have charted the course for the growth and development of its oil region and other parts of the country. The custodian elite should have served as an anchor for establishing and maintaining sustainable economic freedom and livelihoods, with due recognition of the prevailing environment characterised by widespread poverty, declining living standards and oil rent distributional inequity-induced socio-political conflicts.

It is worth expanding on previous accounts of crude oil production and export in Nigeria to appreciate the magnitude of her oil wealth. Oil in Nigeria was first discovered in commercial quantity in Oloibiri, in present day Bayelsa State in the Niger Delta region in 1956 by an Anglo-Dutch consortium, Shell D'Arcy which later became Shell BP. The first export took place two years later after the initial discovery. Ownership of the oil was vested in the Crown by the Minerals Act of 1958. Other Transnational Oil Corporations (TNOCs) such as Mobil, Safrap (later became Elf), Agip, Gulf, Texaco, and so on acquired different concessions at various times; and since, became major actors in the Nigerian oil industry. Under the concession agreements, the companies acquired the right to explore and prospect for oil within given acreages at their own expense and risk, subject to payment of fixed annual rents plus royalties based on the assessment of the tonnage of oil extracted.

At independence in 1960, Nigeria inherited an oil industry under the firm grip of TNOCs, because the state lacked the technological know-how and managerial skills necessary for the operation and maintenance of the sector; as a result, the status quo was maintained. Arrangement was made for the continuous flow of petroleum profit tax into the government coffers, because ownership of the oil and similar natural resources remained vested in the state. It became vested in the central Government substituting the Crown at this time by the Minerals Act of 1958. Meanwhile, additional oilfields were being discovered across the Niger Delta region, and production capacity increased except during the 1967-1970 Biafra war when production was obstructed.

The Organisation of Petroleum Exporting Countries (OPEC) was created in 1960 out of the need to check the powers of TNOCs in the global oil industry. Nigeria attended the OPEC Conference in 1964 as an observer country. Prior to becoming a member in 1971, Nigeria started adopting OPEC's terms in its oil industry. For example, OPEC Resolution NO. XVI.90 of 1968 obligated members to acquire 51% of the equity interests of TNOCs operating in their countries by 1982, and to participate actively in all aspects of oil operations. The resolution coincided with the international pressure to permit countries to exercise permanent sovereignty over their natural resources.

As a result, Nigeria promulgated the Petroleum Decree of 1969 repealing the Minerals Oil Ordinance of 1914. The Decree vested the entire ownership and control of all petroleum in, under or upon any land in the state. Oil under the territorial waters of Nigeria or found in, under, or upon any land which forms part of the continental shelf became owned by the state. The state also reviewed the terms of the existing concessions and instead of providing a single grant, it introduced three types of grants: Oil Exploration Licence (OEL), Oil Prospecting Licence (OPL), and Oil Mining Lease (OML). The Decree further stipulated that only Nigerian citizens or companies incorporated in Nigeria may be granted rights to OEL, OPL or OML. The Petroleum (Drilling and Production) Regulations of the same year directed the oil companies to indigenise their workforce by 70% within seven years and the balance within the shortest possible time. Already, the Companies Decree of 1968 had required the TNOCs to register as Nigerian companies thereby giving government more control over them.

The 1970s witnessed growth of the oil industry as well as government's participation therein. Though some have argued that rapid exploitation of crude oil fuelled this robust economic trend and optimistic prospects concerning economic development and social progress. The government established the state-owned oil company,

Nigerian National Oil Corporation (NNOC) in April 1971, shortly before the country joined OPEC. In addition to marketing government's share of the oil to foreign consumers, NNOC was granted right to explore and prospect for oil like other companies. The grant covered all areas not covered by existing rights and all such areas as might be relinquished to the government from time to time. The grant was not limited by time. The company was expected to develop its own manpower; to encourage indigenous private participation in supporting services; to construct and lay pipes for the delivery of oil and allied resources; to diversify into areas like petrochemicals and fertilizers, and so on.

The Nigerian state acquired a 33.33% participation interest in Nigerian Agip Oil Company in April 1971 as part of its participation drive. An earlier concession agreement had made provision to that effect. Likewise, the government acquired a 35% interest in Safrap as a condition for resumption of operations after the Biafra war. Two years later, it acquired 35% interest in Shell-BP, Mobil and Gulf respectively. By July 1979, Nigeria through the state-owned oil company (NNOC) had acquired up to 60% participation in each of the following companies: Agip, Elf, Gulf, Mobil, Pan Ocean, Shell BP, and Texaco. Its participation in Shell BP rose to 80% following nationalisation of British interest in the company in August 1979. These measures ushered in the regime of participation or joint venture agreements between the government and the TNOCs thereby marking the end of the concession era. It also signified the beginning of what has been referred to as the 'state-global capital alliance' in the Niger Delta of Nigeria.

In 1975, the Ministry of Petroleum Resources was merged with NNOC to give birth to the Nigerian National

Petroleum Corporation (NNPC). NNPC has wider powers than NNOC and oversees all the contracts entered into by the government and the TNOCs. It underwent several structural changes over the years. Its oil production capacity through its subsidiary, the Nigerian Petroleum Development Company (NPDC), increased having established its own seismic crew in 1978 and a second one in 1983, making at least ten offshore commercial discoveries by 1986. By 1990, joint venture production accounted for 96% of total crude oil production and out of this, NNPC's equity share was about 1.7 million barrels per day. Despite the large oil earnings from its soil, the Niger Delta remains one of the poorest regions on earth. Paradoxically, an oil-rich region where most of the people are poor due to the failure of the state political elite to individually and collectively carry out their responsibility and uphold their obligation to society. An obligation that demands the ability to plan, to organise, to order or reorder and above all to make sacrifices for the maximum benefit of all on the part of the state custodian elite. The Midas touch of oil on the economy and people of the Niger Delta in terms of rapid achievement of material prosperity and progress has proved illusory.

****

State ownership of oil and other natural resources is reflected in the 1999 Nigeria Federal Constitution. The vesting provision of s. 44 (3) state

"the entire property in and control of all minerals, mineral oils and natural gas in, under or upon any land in Nigeria or in, under or upon the territorial waters and the Exclusive Economic Zone of Nigeria shall vest in the Government of the Federation and shall be managed in

75

such manner as may be prescribed by the National Assembly (federal parliament)".

This is similar to the provisions contained within section 1 of the Petroleum Act 1969 as well as the Exclusive Economic Zone Act 1978, which vested the Federal Government exclusive rights over the exploration of natural resources of the sea-bed, the subsoil and superjacent waters of the Exclusive Economic Zone.

The level of crude oil production and export is largely determined by demand and of course the technological capacity for more exploration and development. Above all, is the availability of the explorable resources. The growth of Nigeria's oil production has been very impressive. Average production rate was 5000 barrels per day in 1958. Production of about 1.8 million barrels in 1958 rose to about 16.8 million barrels in 1961; about 43.9 million in 1964; and about 116.5 million barrels in 1967. Quantity exported followed a similar growth pattern. As at 1965, there were 3 billion barrels of proven oil reserves.

It was in the 1970s that Nigeria launched itself as one of the important oil producers of the world having regard to its scale of production. It was from 1970 that daily average production exceeded 1 million barrels. Yearly production rate increased to about 558.8 million barrels in 1971; hitting 823.3 million barrels in 1974; with a slight reduction to 766 million barrels in 1977; but picked up to 841.2 million barrels in 1979. As a result of more exploration spurred by high global demand, Nigeria recorded 20.2 billion barrels of proven crude oil reserves in 1975. The bulk of quantity produced was exported throughout the period. Oil exports rose to over 90% of total exports in 1979.

Production decreased in the 1980s with an average 2.3% share of the total world daily production as opposed to the 3.8% share in the 1970s. Between 1981 and 1988, yearly production was in the region of 450 to 540 million barrels. This was due to the economic slump of the decade. Large-scale production resumed towards the end of the decade and saw a steady increase of 828 million barrels to 918 million barrels annually between years 2000 and 2005. By 2008, average daily production stood at 2.5 million barrels. During this time, there was a total of 606 oilfields in the Niger Delta out of which 355 were onshore while 251 offshore. Nigeria became the largest oil producer in Africa, second to Venezuela in OPEC outside the Middle East.

Of equal importance is the fact that crude oil goes along with associated gas. Thus, the more crude oil produced, the more quantity of gas produced. This meant that the Niger Delta as a result of its oil resources is also rich in natural gas. Non-associated gas also exists independent of associated gas. Estimated reserves of natural gas as of 2015 stood at 180 trillion cubic feet (Tcf) making Nigeria ninth in the world in terms of endowment. Associated gas represents roughly 80% of the total natural gas reserves. However, until recently, over 90% of it was flared by the TNOCs in the course of crude oil production. The cost of exploiting natural gas as an alternative energy source (it requires liquefication before being used) was thought to be far higher than the benefit especially since the local demand was insignificant. However, with the Associated Gas Re-injection Decree of 1979, the government sought to halt gas flaring and devised ways by which associated gas could be utilised commercially. But penalties against offending companies were hardly enforced and so large-scale flaring continued into the mid 1990s where 76% of total production was flared. By 2006, about 40% was flared with only 12% re-injected.

To improve the situation, a proposal for the exportation of liquefied gas to places like the US, Japan and Europe where there was high demand thereof was approved earlier under the Fourth National Development Plan (1975 – 1980). The government embarked on the Liquefied Natural Gas Project aimed at constructing a plant at Bonny with a total capacity of 8 billion cubic metres per year. After being on the drawing board since 1976, a joint venture agreement between NNPC and Shell, Agip and Elf led to the formation of the Nigeria Liquefied Natural Gas Limited in 1985 to see to the realisation of the project.

The project was planned to be completed by 1990 but it was only in 1999 that the first export of liquefied gas was made. In effect, Nigeria had strengthened its foreign exchange earning out of the Niger Delta by providing an additional or alternative energy source. The Nigerian Gas Company, a subsidiary of NNPC, became the local marketer and distributor of liquefied gas. By 2012, there were 182 trillion cubic feet of proven natural gas reserves in Nigeria making it the ninth largest in the world. Despite Nigeria's large oil and gas wealth generated from the Niger Delta, the oil minorities missed out on the enormous rent from oil and gas exploitation. This is because its custodian elite had failed to find common cause across ethnicities and define the minimum terms and conditions for the safety, security, growth and prosperity of the people. When the elite abdicates its role, the society fails and such has been the case of the Niger Delta – Nigeria's big heart.

It is hardly contentious to conclude that Nigeria's oil wealth generated earnings worth hundreds of billions of dollars. It was from 1970 that oil export revenue for Nigeria started outweighing export revenue from other sectors, agriculture being hitherto the main sector. Percentage of oil export revenue for the year was 57.48% of total (oil and non-oil) export revenues and it steadily grew to 96.13% in 1980, 97.01% by 1990, dropped to 75.77% in 2000 but rose again to 94.15% in 2007. Total oil export value as a percentage of the total (oil and non-oil) export value for the period 1970 – 2007 was 93.05%.

Oil price per barrel rose from $3.4 in 1973 to $41 by the end of 1981. Nigeria's external reserves bounced back in 1979 to over N3.250 billion and reaching N5.648 billion in 1980. The 1979 Iranian Revolution led to a rise in oil prices such that Nigeria recorded an estimated $15.6 billion and $25 billion export values for 1979 and 1980 respectively. Production slowed down in the mid-1980s and price for the Nigerian oil plummeted to $35.50 per barrel in early 1982, yet the value became impressive again except during the second half of the decade when the barrel price came down to about $10 per barrel. The reduction of external reserves during the first half of the decade to an initial $4.5 billion and then to $3 billion can only be explained by the political elite.

As the country approached the 1990s, export values rose following a rise in production and prices spurred by the 1989 Iraqi invasion of Kuwait and the 1990-91 Gulf War which followed the invasion. After this, the annual export value for Nigeria was between $11 billion and $14.8 billion; entering the new millennium with a fortune in the region of $20 billion and hitting over $32 billion in 2004. At the beginning of 2004, a barrel was about $30 outside OPEC's desired $22-28 price band hitting

$46.61 by October. Nigeria's benchmark price for the year was $25, a situation which enabled her to save over $3.2 billion as excess revenue for the year, and raise its foreign reserve to $12.4 billion. The external reserve at end of 2005, despite the Niger Delta oil conflict, stood at $32 billion. In 2005, Nigeria revised the benchmark price for a barrel of oil to $30 whereas the average price for Nigerian oil was $55.18. $11 billion was saved as excess crude oil revenue.

The 2006 benchmark price was set at $33, a 9% rise from the previous year. OPEC's price was set at $61.08 though the market price fluctuated between $65 and $68 per barrel. The outbreak of the Israeli/Hezbollah war on 12th July 2006 heightened tensions already created by Iran's nuclear enhancement ambition and oil prices instantly rose to about $75 per barrel. The ceasefire brokered by the United Nations (UN) resolution effective on 14th August brought the prices downward by $1.81 to $73.82 per barrel. It was expected that excess oil revenue in Nigeria for the year 2006 would exceed the $33 billion the government had projected. OPEC's Reference Basket (ORB) for 2007 was $69.08 per barrel but the price rose to $85.07 per barrel in the final quarter of the year.

In the first quarter of 2008, the price of oil per barrel reached just over $100. When tensions heightened again over Iran's nuclear programme in the second half of the year, the price per barrel rose to over $130. Nigerian barrel of crude oil (Bonny Light) in particular sold at $127.99 in May 2008, $138.74 in June, and £141.86 in July according to Central Bank of Nigeria (CBN) 2008 statistics. The rise in the value of oil means added income for Nigeria. Between 1970 and 2007, Nigeria's total value of oil exports stood at $571.911 billion. The Nigeria Federal Office of Statistics in 2004 stated that "performance of the oil and gas sector is the most influential single force that propelled [Nigeria's] economic growth".

In recent years, despite the violence and instability in the oil region, total petroleum and other liquids production according to the US Energy Information Administration, in thousand barrels per day (bpd) and yearly accruing revenue stood at:

2010 – 2,459 bpd ($70 billion),
2011 – 2,555 bpd ($99 billion),
2012 – 2,525 bpd ($94 billion),
2013 – 2,372 bpd ($84 billion),
2014 – 2,428 bpd ($77 billion),
2015 – 2,322 bpd ($52 billion).

All these from Nigeria's big heart - the Niger Delta, but with little or nothing to show for it.

****

In 2004, the federal government created an Excess Crude Account as a savings account managed by the federal ministry of finance where all revenue from oil export above the budgeted oil price is deposited and periodically shared among the three tiers of government to fund special projects. Oil revenue allocation has been an issue of constant debate since independence in Nigeria. Though control of the oil resources lies in the federal government, the oil revenues derived therefrom had all along been shared between or among the tiers of government according to formulae which varied from time to time. The two key issues borders on derivation, that is how much revenue oil producing states should keep; and allocation, that is determining how the balance after derivation should be divided between the federal government, states and local government areas.

The history of revenue allocation in pre-independence Nigeria begins with the report of Sir Sydney Phillipson in 1947; the report was on how the revenue raised by the central government should be allocated for expenditure by the regional authorities. The central government had full power on all revenues and allocates revenue to the regions on the basis of derivation. The Phillipson Commission recommended two principles of revenue sharing among the regions – derivation and even development.

As part of the constitutional review processes in 1951, a report on revenue allocation was produced and signed by Professor J.R. Hicks and Sir Sydney Phillipson. The report retained the derivation principle and regional needs, and for the first time introduced the principle of independent revenue. The 1951 Constitution also established a quasi-federal system and gave the regions some power to impose taxes and legislation and appropriate money for specific purposes. Towards independence, there was the need for a new revenue allocation formula, in view of the fact that new regions were created and they needed a level of financial independence if they must function politically. Consequently, in 1953 after the constitutional conference, Sir Louis Chick was appointed to head another revenue allocation commission. He recommended the retention of the existing independent revenues and the extension of the derivation principle to the whole of the centrally generated revenues for allocation to regions.

The Sir Jeremy Raisman Commission on revenue allocation was set up in 1958, to look into the perceived inadequacies of the Chick commission's revenue allocation formula, which included among others the deficiencies in the application of the principles of derivation and the inadequate proportion of the independent revenues for the regions. The Raisman Commission retained the principle of derivation, the fiscal autonomy of the states alongside that of the federal government, and allocated a certain percentage of the mining rents to the federal government and the regions in the following ways; (a) 50% to the regions of origin – based on the principle of derivation, (b) 20% to the federal government, and (c) 30% to the Distributable Pool Account (DPA) to be shared among the regions as follows; North – 40%, East – 31% and West – 24%. The Raisman Commission formula recognises the issue of national unity rather than empowering federating unit(s) at the expense of others.

The Binns Commission was the first revenue allocation commission set up post-independence. Like the Raisman Commission, it maintained the principle of derivation (50% to the regions of origin, 15% to the federal government, and an increase in the Distributable Pool Account (DPA) from 30% to 35%) for sharing of mining rents and royalties; the fiscal independence and national interest were also maintained. However, the first military government that came into power in January 1966 abolished democratic rule and enforced a more centralist structure. By 1967, Nigeria was divided into twelve states that had no autonomy like the former regions, with the federal government at the centre. In 1968, the Dina interim revenue allocation review committee, headed by Mr I.O. Dina, was set up. Among its recommendations was a uniform tax legislation for the country, harmonisation of the pricing of Marketing Board Produce and the financing of all higher education by the federal government. The Dina Committee's recommendations were rejected by the military regime. It felt the report went beyond the mandate given to the committee, and given the country was at the time in the middle of a civil war. Meanwhile, the military government continued with the Binns revenue formula, and later promulgated Decree No. 13 of 1970 which increased revenue allocation to the federal government. The federal government distinguished between onshore and offshore oil revenue. The share of the states of origin in on-shore mining rents and royalties was reduced from 50% derivation to 45%, and that of the federal government from 15% to 5%. However, the federal government allocated to itself 100% of off-shore mining rents via the Off-Shore Oil Revenues Decree No. 9 of 1971 sub-section 2(a) which vested the ownership and title to the territorial waters and continental shelf in the federal government, and stipulated that all royalties, rents and other revenues deriving there from, is accrued to the federal government.

These changes brought about discontent between the oil producing states and the federal government, because the federal government reneged on its civil war time promise to the oil producing states that the principle of derivation will continue to form an important part of the revenue allocation formula. The Aboyade Commission was therefore set up in 1977 as a technical committee to the 1979 Constitution Drafting Committee (CDC) to advice the CDC on the issues of revenue allocation as the nation prepared to return to democratic rule. Its report jettisoned completely the principle of derivation and recommended the consolidation of all federally collected revenue, to be shared based on the following percentages; federal government 57%, state governments 30%, local governments 10% and special grants accounts to be administered by the federal government 3%. It also created the State Joint Accounts to be administered by individual state government. The Aboyade Commission's revenue allocation formula could not be administered by the Shagari Administration, because the Constituent Assembly (Parliament) rejected the report due to its high technicalities; in the sense that it recommended certain indices for revenue allocation that could not be agreed on by members of the parliament.

The federal government went ahead and set up another commission, the Okigbo Commission, to review the revenue allocation formula. The commission recommended the following: federal government 53%, state governments 30%, local governments 10% and special funds 7%. The special funds were further divided into: Federal Capital Territory (FCT) initial development 2.5%, ecological problems 1%, special problem of Mineral Producing Areas 2.0%, and revenue equalisation fund 1.5%. The federal government modified and adopted the commission's proposals ignoring the minority views of the members of the commission from the Niger Delta region.

The recommendations of the Okigbo Commission was declared null and void by the Nigerian Supreme Court on 2nd October 1981. The judgement was made on the importance of the dissenting minority views, and on the suit instituted against the government for increasing the federal government share of the oil revenue while de-emphasising the principle of derivation (by the former Bendel State government comprising the present Edo and Delta oil producing states). After the Supreme Court ruling, the National Assembly (Parliament) passed the Revenue Act of 1981 which came into effect in 1982. It recommended the following Federation Account sharing: federal government 55%, state governments 35%, and local governments 10%. The federal government's 55% included the 4.5% special fund it administers comprising

1% ecological fund, 2% derivation and 1.5% development of oil mineral producing areas. There was another military coup on 31st December 1983 which brought back the military to power. The military adjusted the revenue formula four times between the years 1984 to 1992.

Nigeria returned to civilian rule in 1999 as a federation of 36 states, 774 local governments and a federal capital territory in Abuja. The new 1999 Constitution provided for the federation to maintain an account called the Federation Account into which all revenues collected by the federal government shall be paid. Any amount standing to the credit of the account shall be distributed among the three tiers of government according to a formula to be determined by the National Assembly. Any formula shall take into account equality of states, population, land mass, revenue generation and so on, provided that the derivation principle constantly reflect at least 13% of the revenue accruing to the Federation Account directly from any natural resources (s. 162 [1] [2] [3]). Inspite of the provisions by the new constitution, the debate over oil revenue share did not seem to be settled as the oil producing communities and the people of the Niger Delta continue to agitate for an upward review of the 13% derivation to an acceptable percentage between the range of 25% to 50%. Despite the creation of the Ministry for Niger Delta in September 2008, the issue of revenue allocation is yet to be settled. All these amidst the paradox of underdevelopment in the resource-rich Niger Delta – Nigeria's big but broken heart.

From the foregoing, one can deduce why competition for political power in Nigeria has become nasty and violent, because access to political power is seen as an avenue to easy oil rent. The impact of this on the collective thinking of the elite as a group towards any threat to the free flow of oil in the Niger Delta can only be imagined. The violent nature of the petro-politics in the Niger Delta where militarisation and repression has been the order of the day, both under military and civilian regimes is centred around the exploitation and distribution of oil wealth. At the receiving end of the state (mis)management of its oil resources are the oil minorities of the Niger Delta. A people that has seen their supposed natural blessing turned to a 'curse' by a repressive state. The oil that was supposed to be a tool for national development, has now turned out to be a nemesis.

Chapter 6 –

Calming the Storm

Revolutions often get hijacked by people pursuing parochial agenda. Such is the case with the Niger Delta where a just struggle has been turned negative due to the actions of those less concerned about what the actual Niger Delta issue is all about. Theirs remain assurances of pecuniary benefits through questionable pipeline security contracts, illegal crude oil bunkering and theft. The unholy mix between insurgency and criminality evidenced by the involvement of armed groups in hostage-taking, siphoning of oil from pipelines and the illicit sale in unconventional markets, illegal oil refining and trading, pipelines vandalism, as well as the proliferation of criminal groups disguised as militants, has promoted the view that the conflicts in the Niger Delta are driven by the greed of the actors. Too bad that the 'beautiful ones' are no longer around.

Contemporary conflicts in the oil delta to some degree are instigated by political and traditional elite who are clamouring for a greater share of oil revenues to embezzle. Elite fought by youths interested in sharing pay-offs from the state, Transnational Oil Corporations (TNOCs) or tapping into the illicit gains from oil theft. Blowing up oil pipelines for the purpose of a genuine struggle for equity by Niger Delta militants cannot be totally dismissed as being ineffective. It draws national and international attention to the plight of a minority, who would otherwise not have been listened to by the majority feasting with gluttony on the God-given resources of Nigeria's coastal dwellers. However, when there is no clear-cut agenda-pursuing group among those claiming to be fighting for the people, it means they have simply hijacked a quality platform to pursue personal and criminal agenda.

Militant youths are now canon fodder manipulated by shrewd elite. There is a crisis of leadership and a widening gap between elite, insurgents and their communities. This complex nature of youth militancy in the oil delta is now apparent, especially when one considers how militants use petro-capitalism, even as they resist its consequences for their communities. The evidence of militant connections to the various levels of the oil complex – military, government, TNOCs and local politicians is vast. Today, youth militants in the oil delta utilise the very structures that allowed and created the devastation of the Niger Delta as a means to sustain their activity and to fight against it. This is the central contradiction in militant behaviour: the symbiosis of resistance and accommodation. The symbiosis describes the way in which militancy emerges out of the socio-political and economic consequences of petro-capitalism, and in direct opposition to the different axes along which this is represented (environmental and economic degradation of oil extraction by TNOCs, state repression, local elite complicity and self-enrichment). Yet they connects strongly to the oil complex in order to use the clientelist networks of petro-capitalism to ensure livelihoods and fund continued resistance. It is this contradiction that has made the behaviour and rhetoric of youth militants so difficult to understand, and indeed what has led it to be woefully characterised as being greedy rather than being aggrieved.

****

Several suggestion have been put forward for an alternative conflict and security management approach in the Niger Delta region. For any approach to be viable, it will need to incorporate a mix of a top-down and a bottom-up approach due to the changing nature of threats in the oil delta. The conflict and security management strategy must be proactive and reactive given that threats and opportunities are constantly evolving. The conflict and security management strategy must also adapt to the context of the strategic environment. More importantly, any proposed strategy should accommodate the participation of the civil society as stakeholders in the peace process. This is of particular importance because in Nigeria, the civil society has been systematically excluded from supporting social inclusion for sustainable development and national security by the political elite.

The proposed framework in this book is designed to bring all stakeholders in the Nigerian and Niger Delta security project together. In doing so, both the state and public security needs would be taken into account to a certain degree, bearing in mind that human, state and national security are complementary rather than contradictory. When one is protected, the other is assured. Therefore, a tripartite conflict management/security framework that will involve the Nigerian political elite, Non-Governmental Organisations (NGOs) and community leaders as actors from the larger civil society is hereby outlined through an 'Actors Role and Two Action Levels' (ARTAL) security framework. The ARTAL framework has been originally designed and developed by the author. It has been initiated from the wealth of knowledge gained during his doctoral research and strengthened by the research findings.

ARTAL

Actors: maintaining security in the Niger Delta can be complicated due to the array of actors involved. It can be even more complicated if the actors have divergent interests as it is today, which could impinge on the successful outcome of the security agenda. While these interests might be concealed or clearly manifested, a conflict and security framework clearly designed to accommodate different stakeholders interests will result in optimum security. The state political elite, NGOs and community leaders need to work together in building a culture of peace in the Niger Delta and probably elsewhere in Nigeria. Peace can only be sustained by an array of people who perform various functions at different times. Through their sustained actions as security actors, the political elite, community leaders and NGO officials can transform the civil-military relation in the Niger Delta from a confrontational one to a partnership one. The state political elite should mobilise all other elite networks. The tripartite elite group of the military both serving and retired, the economic elite that comprises entrepreneurs, industrialists and businessmen, and the professional elite whose skills and knowledge serves as the engine house of governance can create a common security by facilitating friendly relations with other security stakeholders in the Niger Delta through peacemaking and peacekeeping efforts.

Role: there already exists an array of NGOs in and outside Nigeria championing the cause of the oil minorities of the Niger Delta through advocacy, campaigning and public enlightment. The activism has paid off in the past and the NGOs can still play a crucial role in national peacebuilding by assisting in establishing new forms of governance at local, state and federal levels; and in helping the demobilisation of insurgents and implementation of longer term security measures.

Furthermore, community leaders like local tribal chiefs, religious and ethnic associations leaders, women and cooperative groups leaders and youth organisations officers, can volunteer to provide activities that will sustain the peacemaking, peacekeeping and peacebuilding efforts from the bottom-up rather than just from the top-down. Although media attention have always been on governing political elite to create an enabling security environment in the delta through a top-down governing process, evidence abound of a rich vein of locally-based peacebuilding actions through local movements that has had national and transnational effects. A good example is the significant role played by community groups in the Arms for Development (AfD) approach adopted in Sierra Leone in 2002 under the auspices of United Nations Development Programme (UNDP) and the Sierra Leonean government. The programme that encouraged giving up arms in exchange for communal projects is a direct contrast to the presidential amnesty programme implemented in the Niger Delta, which paid cash for arms buybacks from militants. While the AfD benefitted the entire community, the amnesty programme in the Niger Delta seemed to have only benefitted the insurgent leaders and some of their militias. The civil society could have been engaged to sensitise the Niger Delta militants on the need to voluntarily surrender arms in exchange for immediate and visible public facilities.

Action Level 1: level one actions under the ARTAL security framework places much responsibility on the political elite. It requires them to set up a process of peacemaking by initiating mediation and negotiation channels with other stakeholders such as the local leaders and NGOs. This by no means imply that the state will jettison its peacekeeping responsibility, which entails deployment of security apparatus especially since military troops are already in the zone. However, there will come a time at a later stage of the security framework, when trust is fully built between the civil society and the governing regime. Therefore, military presence will have to be whittled down to the minimum level. At this level, NGOs could contribute to the peace-making process through a national peacebuilding effort by encouraging what could be termed 'people exchange', which would involve building relationships between individuals, government officials, ethnic, religious and educational organisations that can act as a positive force for good.

Community leaders will also have a responsibility to contribute to local peacebuilding efforts by providing volunteering assistance in the area of information dissemination, as the people might initially be suspicious seeing uniformed men around. The peace effort at this level of the ARTAL framework is based on the notion that "the best providers of development assistance are probably voluntary people's organisations engaging in people-people rather than expert-expert dialogues, providing assistance closer to basic needs, and being ready to accept reciprocity".

Action Level 2: level two actions of the ARTAL security framework entails a multifaceted approach. Aside promoting dialogue between the different stakeholders through high level diplomacy stipulated in level one, the political elite should work towards transformation of governance at local and state levels in the delta region.

The mode of governance currently perceived to be bad, has been the major driving factor of the Niger Delta oil conflict, leading to tensions and instability. The perception emerging from the structural factor due to the way government and the political economy operate in the oil region has further created provocating factors that has sparked violent agitations and armed conflict. Addressing the drivers of unrest is vital at this stage of the security framework in order to curb the deterioration of the provocation factors such as securitisation. Doing otherwise might jeopardise the dialogue already initiated and throw the region back into a destructive cycle of instability witnessed prior to the implementation of the amnesty programme, and as seen in early 2016.

To address the issue of bad governance, the political elite can accelerate the passing of the Petroleum Industry Bill (PIB), which is still pending in the legislature. This proposed political and legal framework for the Nigerian oil industry is meant to readjust the political economy of oil exploration and management, but has stalled in the parliament of the country for the past seven years due to opposition from TNOCs and their allies in the Legislative and Executive arms of government. General opinion suggest that oil companies policies and practices need revamping to be up to date with modern practices and international standard.

Further, at this level of the ARTAL framework, the political elite should address some deeper structural issues such as revisiting the issue of environmental governance in the Niger Delta, tackling corruption at all levels of government, adopting poverty alleviation measures through job creation, execute physical infrastructure projects and complete all abandoned projects in the region. Although research findings indicate that majority of the oil communities favoured having greater control of their resources either through the derivation allocation, to enable them to self-develop. However, by embarking on an accelerated program of massive infrastructure development, the oil communities will feel the closeness of government to them as host communities and be receptive to other state policies in maintaining security. It should be noted that there are government agencies already in place to carry out some of these functions such as the Economic and Financial Crime Commission (EFCC) for fighting corruption, and the Niger Delta Development Commission (NDDC) for administering infrastructural development. However, the issue has been on whether the political elite have the will to carry out the reforms?

Another perspective to the security-development nexus in the Niger Delta is the issue of peacekeeping/enforcement on the part of the state. The historical antecedents of the military Joint Task Force (JTF) in the Niger Delta made the inhabitants to perceive them as 'occupation forces' meant to protect big business, and as such were unreceptive towards them. But the level of criminality in the region today has changed the feeling to that of ambivalence towards the JTF, because the local residents' perception of the militias have also changed. Some inhabitants of the oil delta rather than perceive the militias as freedom fighters as the case was in the early days of the struggle, now see them as criminals and opportunists alongside the political elite. This experience might open a window of opportunity for both peacebuilding and peace enforcement efforts on the part of the state. The state can streamline the amount of military personnel who are already in the region while assuring the locals that the remaining troops are meant to safeguard their human security. To canvass for total military withdrawal at this stage of the conflict will be tantamount to calling for a political suicide of the state and its 'investing partners' in the oil region. Evidence on ground suggest the region is a hot-bed of violence and criminality, and no one seems to argue that the idea behind human security is security for all to attain optimum security. Everyone agrees that security has to be provided by the state for real development to take place in the oil delta. However, as the level of insecurity improves, further routine withdrawal of forces should be made until it gets to the minimum level that will be determined by circumstances.

With the ongoing re-orientation in the Nigerian military on the need for interpersonal and community liaison skills that will capture the 'hearts and minds' of the people, the security apparatus can endear themselves to the locals and improve the civil-military relation in the region. This will also impact on the state-civil society relation. To achieve this positive civil-military relation, civilianising military functions is recommended whereby the military will assist in development tasks such as helping out in civil defence during natural disasters.

The actions for NGOs at this level of the ARTAL security framework, with its peacekeeping role traditionally viewed from a military function perspective, may involve conflict resolution, information dissemination, governance monitoring, retraining of ex-combatants under the amnesty programme and setting up a process of societal healing that will involve local leaders at communal level. Observers have previously queried the wisdom in using solely combat troops for peacekeeping operations because of their battlefield training orientation. According to popular opinion, rather than saddle combat troops with peacemaking duties that may include social functions, civilian groups or the police force could be utilised to perform such functions effectively. NGOs outside and in the oil region can support state reform efforts by engaging with local communities regularly and informing them of employment opportunities and open bid contracts available. Until recently, this have been communicated to and enjoyed by local elite and insurgent leaders. But by strengthening the communities through broad stakeholder involvement in the developmental process, the people will have trust in the new inclusive approach and transmit this in a reciprocal manner to the state.

The re-integration of the ex-combatants under the amnesty programme can also be sustained by support from NGOs. Skills training, apprenticeship and job placement should not just be the prerogative of government, other stakeholders should get involved as well through public-private partnership schemes. These attractive alternatives can serve as strong disincentives to crime and encourage a culture of peace in the region and elsewhere in the country. What the foregoing suggest is that NGOs can serve as a peace army. Equally important at this level in the framework is for the NGOs to encourage citizen monitoring and reporting on governance and security practices. In the context of the Niger Delta, the local communities have been voicing their experience and opinion on issues such as lack of social amenities, environmental quality, human rights abuses and electoral malpractices. They can be further encouraged by the NGOs to uphold this attitude so as to promote transparency and social accountability in governance which will ultimately result to good governance that has been craved for by all.

Furthermore, at level two of the ARTAL security framework is the actions for the local leaders, they should be proactive in their role by helping to boost trust in the new governance and security mode. Evidence abound of how religious leaders and organisations have been at the forefront of peacebuilding efforts in divided and conflicting societies for decades. Such individuals and groups have advocated for non-violent social change and called for space to explore alternatives. The local leaders can provide strong moral ground for their communities to look beyond the past and reach out to the future in order to lay a groundwork for sustainable and enduring peace in the delta. Their task at this level should involve transforming people's perceptions that human security and enduring peace is possible, but requires the contribution and commitment of all stakeholders in the peace process. By doing so, all the stakeholders at level two of the ARTAL security framework would have prepared future generations for peace and stability in the Niger Delta by transforming the present.

None could deny the daunting nature of the security challenges in the Niger Delta and elsewhere in Nigeria. There will be no quick fix, neither would there be eventual winners or losers. To create a strategic environment for peace, the ARTAL analytical alternative conflict management and security framework proposed has demonstrated that several actors will need to be on board and full hands on the deck. With sincerity of purpose of all stakeholders and the will to accept the broader conceptualisation of security as advocated by proponents of human security, a dualistic interpretation of security is achievable and can be operationalised in the oil delta. Improving upon and reforming some social, political, economic and security practices will de-escalate tensions in the oil belt without the coercive instrument of state power been deployed.

The proposed conflict management and security framework has shown that there are alternatives to military-driven strategies, one that is based on 'security-development' nexus. Its focus should be on accelerated development interventions, environmental protection and political rights as against the deployment of the coercive and authoritarian instrument of state power. Given that underdevelopment and bad governance, resulting to environmental degradation due to political elite's laxity in managing the TNOCs, were top key issues observed at the heart of the Niger Delta crisis giving rise to the violent conflict; the state political elite should engage other stakeholders in a collaborative arrangement with sincerity of purpose on the part of the state for a lasting solution to take place.

The modality for achieving this is something that will not only be at the terms of the state, but also at the terms of all the stakeholders involved with a bit of extra mediation effort from independent parties. In conclusion, the ARTAL conflict management and security framework is operable, although requires a security re-orientation and the political will on the part of all the stakeholders to be successful.

It is evidenced that the Nigerian security decision-making body has failed in its ability to prioritise the more pressing security threat between environmental insecurity and civil agitation. This misperception of security and threat have resulted in missed opportunities for national cohesion, subsequently, the direction for meaningful conflict management and security strategies were lost along the way. As a consequence, the domestic security environment became violent for both state and businesses, and state security strategies has ever since been reactive. From a simplistic point of view, one might argue that the Niger Delta imbroglio can only be resolved if the inherent contradictions are fully addressed through economic and socio-political actions, not through military strategy. However, translated in concrete terms that recognises the internal nature of security threats, this book has emphasised the need for a mixture of military and non-military strategies with a clear focus on citizen-centred security to resolve the conflict. It would require auxiliary national resources to be allocated to the region for government to face less crisis of legitimacy, as failure to do so and thus resolve the conflict on time and permanently, will continue to impact on national security and stability in the region. Since a greater part of this book has highlighted that the political elite's preferred conflict management and security strategy has been less than satisfactory, then there is need for a re-direction of national security policy. The starting point is to embrace the civil society as stakeholders in security provision. It will require sacrifices and compromises to be made by all sides for peace and security to return to the delta region and be maintained. This is what the 'ARTAL' security management framework have proposed.

While the author's proposed ARTAL framework did not anticipate for an increase in resource control given this was one of the key demands from the oil communities, it however proposes measures that addresses the issues of underdevelopment, security cooperation, youth unemployment and environmental degradation. The other fact that the proposed ARTAL framework did not rule out all forms of military intervention might make certain people to question the emancipatory and humanistic purpose of the suggested solution. This book cannot be accused of maintaining the status quo because of the numerous changes proposed in security provision, and its articulated inadequacy of traditional national security perspective. A keen observer would admit that the current domestic security environment of the Niger Delta is one that is volatile, violent, nasty and brutish; even to the ordinary inhabitant of the oil region as evidence on ground has shown. The proliferation of different youth groups involving those based on the ideology of marginalisation, while others are simply opportunistic, will surely demand a mix of both 'stick and carrot' approach till the situation improves. The idea that state actors in Nigeria will completely demilitarise the zone right from the onset of peacemaking initiatives can best be described as naive or wishful thinking at worst. The solution however, lies in an integrated conflict management approach, which the ARTAL framework provides.

What is true of Nigeria in the past decade and half specifically in the Niger Delta region need not be true in the coming years. While the security challenges may be dire, they are not insurmountable. Since national security threats under the period studied has proven to be elite determined, then with careful planning and wise leadership, the situation can be resolved. National security should be taken to mean not just the preservation of the small governing elite, but should encompass the protection and preservation of all the component parts of the civil society that includes the citizenry. Individuals and groups have to be protected by the state from all forms of human insecurity that include economic and environmental concerns. Likewise, the state should avoid the use of arbitrary and coercive power to demand for its own security. A well-conceived national conflict management and security strategy that provides coherent part towards the identification, advancement and protection of citizens' interests should be given priority.

Author's Note

The last government administration in Nigeria was divinely ordained to take the Niger Delta to the 'Promised Land', through a return to what the oil minorities negotiated with the Willink Commission before independence in 1960. It did not fulfil that purpose. Instead, the ex-president from the Niger Delta and his cronies ran the country aground.

From the revelations of today, pecuniary concerns were topmost on the Niger Delta's elite and their compromising insurgent leaders' agenda, not equity for their people who have been victims of their natural resource endowment. The elite and insurgents allocated positions and funds to themselves to buy up properties at home and abroad, leaving the suffering local population at the hands of a repressive state. Rather than use the opportunity of a Niger Delta presidency to actualise the dreams of the founding fathers of Movement for the Survival of Ogoni People (MOSOP), the gluttons from the Niger Delta embezzled trillions of naira they got on behalf of the Niger Delta since 1999 when the current dispensation began. How heart-broken the 'beautiful ones' who are no longer around must be in their graves.

Nonetheless, there is no justification for the current government administration in Nigeria to play the vengeance game in dealing with the security challenges in the region. As a total military solution to a crisis in the Niger Delta as learnt earlier will ultimately prove to be inadequate. The chicken is only coming to roost in the Niger Delta as the author observed. There should be a return to the core issues of human insecurity in the oil region. Position, cash or contract appeasement has not in any way resolved the core problems of existential and environmental crises in the Niger Delta. The evil day was merely postponed by the state political elite. Unless the contending issues of equity, resource control, federalism, justice and environmental degradation are addressed, those who throw tokens at the problem can only do so in vain.

I have advanced the argument in this book that oil in the Niger Delta should not only be interpreted as a "curse" or "blessing", or the conflicts emanating from it as being rooted in "scarcity" or "abundance". I have argued that the oil in the region, the role it has played in the socio-politico and economic affairs of the Nigerian state, and its vulnerability to causing conflicts, is mainly functions of the laws, structures and practices guiding the management of the natural resource. Especially the distribution of privileges and opportunities from it, and not the circumstances or nature of its physical existence. My position is that a greater percentage of the oil resources should be distributed and managed in ways that benefit the oil-producing communities.

In my view, poverty at its root in the Niger Delta is bred by unequal power relations, the structural and systematic allocation of resources among different groups in society and their differential access to power and the political process. The distorted distribution of the oil/nation's wealth has resulted in the enrichment of a minority (mostly the elite and their associates) at the expense of an impoverished citizenry. There is no doubt that the chronic nature of poverty in the Niger Delta and elsewhere in Nigeria has a link to historical and continuing mismanagement of resources, persistent and institutional uncertainty primarily occasioned by military rule, weak rule of law, decrepit and/or absent

103

infrastructure, weak institutions of state and monumental corruption. Although, there are external factors like the negative impact of globalisation, that are equally culpable, nevertheless, central to the depth of poverty has been poor governance.

On a final note, it is commonly said that we all have a book inside us – a story to tell. But I have to confess that I am a reluctant storyteller. I know the reader will understand how dearly I wish that the events described in these pages had never happened. I was blown apart and dragged down to the depths of despair on my return home to the Niger Delta. As a result, my decision to write this book was born out of wanting to pass on an account of what I observed and experienced to future generations. I want them to know and understand that the Niger Delta conflict is not an outcome of clearly determinable and predictable linear patterns of cause and effect. Rather, it can be viewed from the perspective of an outcome of contingent predisposing factors of which oil as a natural resource is central. This becomes necessary for the fact that the ownership, management and control of oil have been linked and described as the issues underlining the conflict.

I argued that the Niger Delta conflict is a fallout of bad governance, especially as this involves the weakness of administrative structures designed to manage oil resources; the inadequacy of laws and regulations governing the sharing of the endowment; the intricacies of elite politics; and the changing role of civil society. All these I inextricably linked to the complete defectiveness or selective efficiency of the apparatus of natural resource governance in Nigeria.

N.B.

At the point of publication of this book, crude oil has been discovered in commercial quantity in Lagos State of western Nigeria. This brings the number of oil-producing states to ten in the country and higher oil revenue.

Data Source

BP Global (2009) Statistical Review of World Energy 2009. London: BP, pp. 6-24.

CBN (2007) Statistical Bulletin volume 18, December 2007, Abuja: Central Bank of Nigeria (CBN).

CBN (2006) Annual Report and Statement of Accounts, Abuja: Central Bank of Nigeria (CBN).

EIA (2012) US Energy and Information Administration 2012 Nigeria's report. Available at: http://www.eia.gov/countries/analysisbriefs/Nigeria/nigeria.pdf.

Federal Government of Nigeria (1999) Constitution of the Federal Republic of Nigeria. Lagos: Government Press.

Federal Ministry of Finance (2006) Detailed Breakdown of Allocations to Federal, States and Local Governments June 1999 to December 2005. Abuja: Federal Ministry of Finance.

Federal Ministry of Finance and Economic Development (2002) Federal Government Revenue Accounts. Abuja: Federal Ministry of Finance.

FMF/BOF (2008) Fiscal Strategy Paper (Revised Version) of the Federal Government of Nigeria 2009-2011. Abuja: Budget Office of the Federation.

Francis, P., Lapin, D., and Rossiasco, P. (2011) Securing Development and Peace in the Niger Delta: A Social and Conflict Analysis for Change. A publication of the Woodrow Wilson International Center for Scholars. Available at: http:// www.wilsoncenter.org/sites/default/files/AFR.

HDI (2013) 'Human Development Index Report'. Available at: http://hdr.undp.org/sites/default/files/reports.....

HRW (2002) The Niger Delta: No Democratic Dividend. Human Rights Watch Reports. Vol.14, No.7(A). Available at: http://www.hrw.org.

HRW (2000) The Destruction of Odi and Rape in Choba December 22, 1999. Human Rights Watch Reports. Available at: http://www.hrw.org.

HRW (1999) The Price of Oil: Corporate Responsibility and Human Rights Violations in Nigeria's Oil Producing Communities". Human Rights Watch Reports. Available at: http://www.hrw.org.

HRW (1995) The Ogoni Crisis: A Case-Study Of Military Repression In Southeastern Nigeria. Human Rights Watch Reports. Vol. 7, No.5. Available at: http://www.hrw.org.

ICG (2006a) Nigeria: Want in the Midst of Plenty. International Crisis Group Africa Security Report No 113. Available at: http://www.crisisgroup.org.

ICG (2006b) The Swamps of Insurgency: Nigeria's Delta Unrest. International Crisis Group Africa Report. No 113. Available at: http://www.crisisgroup.org.

Julius, P. (2015) Nigerian Political Elite's Perception and Construction of Security Strategies 1999 – 2013: The Case of the Niger Delta Oil Conflict. PhD Thesis, Kingston University, London.

Julius, P. (2014a) 'Re-assessing the Niger Delta Oil Conflict: A Securitisation Perspective', African Journal of Social Sciences, 4(4) pp. 82-94.

Julius, P. (2014b) 'Rethinking Elite Transformation in Contemporary Nigeria', Afro Asian Journal of Social Sciences, 5(1) pp. 1-9.

Julius, P. (2013) 'Investigating Elite Security Dilemma in Nigeria: Issues and Methodology', International Journal of Social Sciences and Humanities Review 4(3) pp. 156-163.

Julius, P. (2011) Security Cooperation in the Gulf of Guinea: A Case Study of the United States Africa Command (AFRICOM) in Nigeria. Unpublished MSc dissertation, Kingston University.

NDDC (2005) Mission Statement, Vision and Strategy of the Niger Delta Development Commission. Port Harcourt: NDDC 1, 5.

NDES (2000) Niger Delta Environmental Survey. Port Harcourt: Shell/IOCs.

NEITI (2009) Audit Report on the Nigerian Oil and Gas Industry 2005. Abuja: Nigeria Extractive Industries Transparency Initiative.

NEITI (2006) Audit Report of the Period 1999-2004. Abuja: Nigeria Extractive Industries Transparency Initiative.

Nigeria Independence Constitution of 1960. Available at: http://www.worldstatesmen.org/nigeria_const1960.pd.

RMAFC (2005) Revenue Mobilization Allocation and Fiscal Commission Law Brochure. Abuja: RMAFC.

UNDP (2006) 'Niger Delta Human Development Report', Abuja. A publication of the United Nations Development Programme.

Willink, Henry (1958) Colonial Office Nigeria. Report of the Willink Commission appointed to enquire into the fears of the oil minorities and the means of allaying them. London: Her Majesty Stationery Office.

** www.hsrhub.org/publications

** Interview/Field Notes.

Appendix - map of Nigeria

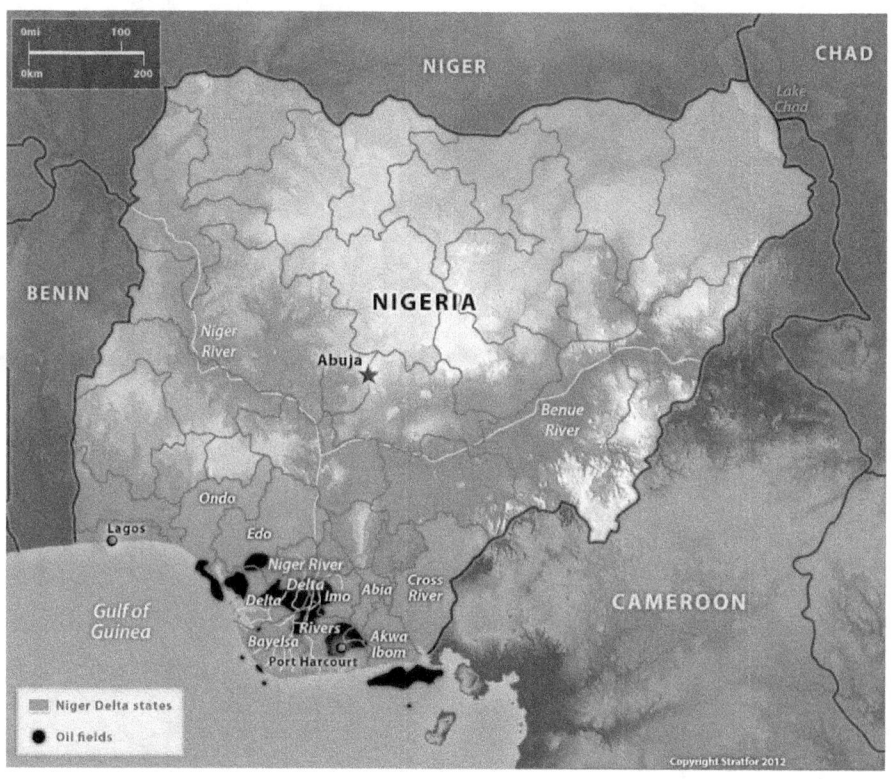